Collaborative Leadership

Collaborative Leadership

Building Capacity through Effective Partnerships

Fern Aefsky

ROWMAN & LITTLEFIELD
Lanham • Boulder • New York • London

Published by Rowman & Littlefield
A wholly owned subsidiary of The Rowman & Littlefield Publishing Group, Inc.
4501 Forbes Boulevard, Suite 200, Lanham, Maryland 20706
www.rowman.com

Unit A, Whitacre Mews, 26-34 Stannary Street, London SE11 4AB

British Library Cataloguing in Publication Information Available

Library of Congress Cataloging-in-Publication Data

978-1-4758-3451-2 (cloth : alk. paper)
978-1-4758-3452-9 (pbk. : alk. paper)
978-1-4758-3453-6 (electronic)

♾ ™ The paper used in this publication meets the minimum requirements of American
National Standard for Information Sciences Permanence of Paper for Printed Library
Materials, ANSI/NISO Z39.48-1992.

Printed in the United States of America

To my wonderful parents, Harold and Selma Heller, who provided me with the support and guidance to go where life led; my sons, Sean and Scott, and husband Carl, for their love and patience; and my colleagues whose knowledge, care, and collaboration made this book possible.

Contents

Foreword

William J. Lennox, Jr.

This book focuses on an important form of leadership the authors have successfully cultivated both within the world of the individual university and among the university and other, seemingly external, stakeholders. **Collaborative leadership** is a pleasant-sounding concept, but insufficiently understood. This book demonstrates the broad variety of benefits that come from collaborative activities that mature into true meaningful and creative partnerships.

People know intuitively that this is common sense. But sometimes even smart, experienced people still have trouble seeing how they can apply collaborative leadership within a large institution that already has its own routines and organizational lines and divisions. The authors of these chapters have mapped out their experiences and detailed the clear benefits that emerge.

First and foremost for a university is the development of the student. Students benefit from partnerships developed by business, education, human services, and criminal justice programs with workplaces and agencies where the objectives are to offer and develop internship placements, to give students the chance to develop real-life knowledge and skills sets that further their learning goals, and to allow students to develop into employees that will meet the needs of agencies and workforces. Students who have discerned their talents and have identified their college major interests naturally gravitate to programs that combine experience with curriculum. When these same students emerge from their respective programs as qualified practitioners, their new employers benefit immediately—whether they are hiring business people, teachers, agency personnel, or law enforcement officers. Our broad society and economy benefit by having well-trained college graduates available to join these critical vocations.

The authors also detail the ways the university itself benefits from the collaborative approach that serves the students so well. Program enrollment stabilizes and expands when students learn which institutions offer the best outcomes. Retention rates improve. Income is more consistent and predictable—attributes that are very important for a university's fiscal profile. Institutions need to be strong financially to keep investing in ideas for improvements, expansions, or new programs. So it is important for university leaders across the organization to know how to create these conditions for success.

Using the collaborative leadership model will also help the institution develop capacity within the institution, drawing on talent already existing within the university workforce. As administrators work together to build programs of shared interest and common goals, their leadership skills evolve. Their enhanced skill sets may prove useful in meeting various university and organizational challenges. And the stronger leaders will be more intellectually and emotionally invested in the success of the university.

—Dr. William J. Lennox, Jr.

Preface

Partnerships in education is not a new concept. However, a renewed focus on various partnerships have become a priority at the national level. This is in part, a result of the 114th Congress (2015) passing the Every Student Succeed Act (ESSA) with mandatory compliance required by all states by the 2017–2018 school year.

Highlights from the new legislation include:

- New federal-state partnerships that provide greater flexibility and funding for districts to support all students in preparation for college and careers;
- Focus on including stakeholders, identified as school leaders, state and district officials, business groups, families and non-profit groups in engagement of stakeholder feedback;
- Importance of transparency and stakeholder engagement in the spirit of collaboration to improve demonstrated student achievement;
- Design of an implementation plan that includes representatives of all stakeholders impacted by the law, including state policy makers; board of education members at the state and local level; teachers; principals; parents; related service providers; community based organizations; institutes of higher education; and employers and business organizations.

The issue of creating and sustaining successful partnerships was evident in research between 1992 and 2008, but family involvement in schools was the key component (Datnow and Stringfield, 2000; Fullan, Hill and Crevola, 2006; Sergiavanni, 1992; Weiss and Stephen, 2009).

While this is one aspect that will be discussed in this book, many other variables support partnerships that engage and develop leaders in K–12 settings. Research has been conducted that identifies characteristics of collaborative work between school and university partnerships that includes impact on teacher and administrator preparation programs, impact on teaching and learning in both the K–12 and university setting, and the importance of community partnerships at both the university and K–12 school levels, including involvement of businesses, non-profit agencies and community groups (Adams, 2015; Ammentorp and Madden, 2014; Gardner, 2011; Petersen and Treagust, 2014; Wasonga, Rari, and Wanzare, 2011).

There are many similarities in different programs that support the fact that leadership skills transcend individual organization or disciplines. There are multiple ways that universities can engage stakeholders that create and support leadership development in all fields, and by gathering those program data, teacher and leader preparation programs offered by universities and colleges can enhance program components and candidate outcomes. These positive outcomes improve student achievement and assist practitioners in their K–12 settings in a variety of ways. Teachers, administrators, families and most importantly students, benefit from collaborative approach to developing leadership skills in teachers and administrators, supported by university programs.

Beyond the requirements of ESSA and schools of education, a focus on university partnerships that facilitate the growth of university program development in schools of business, human services and criminal justice are also well-supported by research (Campbell and Lassiter, 2010; Curwood, Munger, Mitchell, Mackeigan, and Farrar, 2011; Kronick, Lester, and Luter, 2013; Mileski, Mohamed, and Hunter, 2014; Martin, 2015).

Warren Bennis of Harvard described leadership as "Becoming a leader is synonymous with becoming yourself. It is precisely that simple and it's also that difficult" (Ignatius, 2015). At Saint Leo University in San Antonio, Florida, Dr. Arthur Kirk, became the eighth president of what was Saint Leo College in 1997. I asked Dr. Kirk prior to his retirement to identify his leadership qualities and how he was able to turn the college around into a growing university with over sixteen thousand students. Dr. Kirk identified value-based goals and vision, and the internal strength to deal with the execution of the mission and accountability for execution process to achieve those goals. Dr. Kirk identified the process to change the culture and clarify purpose of the organization that led to success. Under Dr. Kirk's tenure at Saint Leo University, he was able to foster various partnerships that enabled programs to grow and set the stage for the next organizational change and improvement cycle.

Dr. William Lenox, lieutenant general (ret) U.S. Army, former Superintendent of West Point, and the current president of Saint Leo University, shared insights on leadership with university participants in the Leadership Saint Leo program (December 2015). He identified leadership keys as a vision that is mission oriented, team building oriented, that focuses on people and communication skills, ethics, courage, and health. He stated his belief that leadership skills can be developed as part of a journey to reach potential of individuals and organizations.

As a school leader in K–12 for more than twenty-five years, and an adjunct (twenty-one years) and now full-time faculty member (four years) of institutes of higher education, the link between initial teacher preparatory and educational leadership programs at universities and practitioners in K–12 settings has long been an area of interest and study. It always surprises me when doing collaborative research and conference presentations with colleagues from the school of business or business world, how perceptions of educators is separated by those colleagues, and they often wonder how educators recognize schools as businesses.

The information presented in this book consists of examples of real partnerships that build leadership capacity through inter- and intradepartmental activities within the university setting. Human services, criminal justice, business, education and community, and business partnerships are shared. Partnerships with school districts through instructional and educational leadership programs and activities are described and how the engagement of all stakeholders provides opportunities for building the capacity of leaders at all levels of each organization are discussed. Family and community partnerships, for all students, including information specific to students with disabilities, are identified as ways of engaging the larger community.

The ability to maximize experiences for students and adults, and create meaningful partnerships with community members and businesses that impact growth for all organizational leaders is a targeted goal of this book. Replication of events shared have been actualized, and it is the authors' belief that by sharing this information other organizational partnerships can be developed and benefit stakeholders in proactive and positive ways.

Chapter One

Building Capacity through University, K–12, and Community Partnerships

Fern Aefsky

Partnerships within and between university programs, educators at the university level, and practitioners in pre-K–12 schools, and with community agencies and businesses help build, enhance, and sustain successful leaders in all disciplines. Practitioners involved in blending content knowledge with practicum experiences are able to use experiences in their workplace to contribute to their work in a global economy.

Leadership development is evident in all disciplines. Much of the support for leadership development is focused in schools of management, yet all disciplines create and develop leaders. The background for leadership theory is driven by psychological theories and is applicable across disciplines (Dweck 2006). Leadership skill development and research is segregated and this book focuses on the skills and characteristics of building capacity of effective leaders in each discipline through partnerships.

Building leadership teams inclusive of all levels of management, faculty, and staff commensurate with organizational goals, mission, and vision supports both individual and team objectives. The importance of partnerships is well-documented in research (Amrein-Beardsley et al. 2013; Wilson 2014). Partnerships with various stakeholders strengthens those leadership teams.

Collaboration of partnership personnel is important, as people identify with the organization to which they belong, and if different organizations, roles, and responsibilities are defined differently. Leaders of each partner organization need to identify aspects of working together so that the combined efforts of the partnership serves each organization's purpose and goals.

Value-based leadership defines the core value of successful partnerships. Cohen (2005) outlined a three step process for leading organizational change:

1

creating a climate for change, engaging and enabling the whole organization, and implementing and sustaining change. This process offers a framework for leaders to include all stakeholders on behalf on improving student achievement and increasing positive learning outcomes.

LEADERSHIP DEVELOPMENT

Regardless of the type of organization, leaders are needed to make things happen, facilitate change, accomplish organizational goals, and develop members of their organization into gaining leadership roles. Think about great leaders in education, organizations, and government that you may have heard about, observed, or experienced. It shouldn't matter what type of organization a leader is part of when you think about characteristics that make that person a great leader. For example, what did you experience or observe that would make you think he or she was a great leader? Did that leader lead by example, dictate what needed to be done, take responsibility for actions, take credit, share credit, or blame others? A great leader does not govern by a single variable. Situations require different leadership actions.

Literature supports multiple types of leadership, including distributive, hierarchal, transformational, transactional, and autocratic or bureaucratic leadership (Barsh and Lavoie 2014; Hewertson 2015; Maxwell 2013). Leadership is often defined as a process of influencing how others think or act and the consequences of those results. One mistake many leaders make is the assumption that only their actions result in leadership attributes. However, the reactions of others create a domino effect of additional emergent leaders in the organization.

Good leaders know when to share power and authority and when decisions must be made. Values and ethics of leadership define the interactions among leaders and those they influence (Aefsky 2015). Examples below are from military, corporate, and educational endeavors and provide a framework for the information presented in this book. The recognition of similarity across disciplines helps set the stage for creating and sustaining successful partnership and developing leaders through those partnerships.

MILITARY

Leader development in the military (army) was described as meeting a need for leaders to gain the necessary skills to effectively lead a complex organization by demonstrating life-long learning, the ability to recognize changing conditions, and when to develop innovative solutions and use critical thinking skills to apply to a variety of potential challenges (Walde, Bundeswehr, and Schwartzman 2011). These authors described the need to achieve stated outcomes and recognize cultural differences in systemic strategies. Assessing organizational needs, facilitating needed change to meet those needs, and implementing new practices are actions that leaders take to reach goals of a mission. Collaboration with partners was highlighted as necessary to work together with collation members.

Hernandez (2010) studied the connection between leadership qualities defined by the U.S. Air Force Officer's Guide related to the transition of military leader to school district leader. She reported that these leadership skills were applicable in all organizations, and described required Air Force Officer's Guide specific qualities of leadership as those required in school districts. These leadership skills included setting goals and expectations of excellence, teamwork (collaboration), flexibility, motivating people, and adjusting leadership style for various situations.

Leaders are developed in the U.S. Air Force Academy through formal training and progressive levels of responsibility (Didier 2012). This researcher investigated connections between student (cadet) leaders and successive leadership pipeline. Mentorships, classes on leadership theory and practice, and definition of mission for leaders are integral parts of this leadership training program.

The U.S. Marines have a similar program of leadership training and focus that have been connected to school administrator training and practice (Logan 2004). Guidance for identifying leadership styles and developing skills are similar to the eleven leadership principles in the U.S. Marine Training Manual.

The Army Management Staff College (AMSC) stated mission is to promote and develop leadership skills and self-efficacy in order to transform leadership development for civilian employees (Godinez and Leslie 2015). This program immerses students in transformational leadership development activities that enable students to transfer learning into the workplace. The result is that army civilians become leaders who have a positive influence in the work environment that enables them to improve organizational entities.

CORPORATE

The Business-Higher Education Forum (BHEF) was formed in 2004 specifically to inform policy on issues of business, higher education, and K–12 schools (Fitzgerald 2006). As a leader in science, technology, engineering, and mathematics (STEM) education, the organization has attempted, through partnerships, to improve student participation and achievement in K–12 systems. A national public education campaign was launched to encourage parents to have their students participate in rigorous STEM programs in K–12 schools, and with university partners, build programs of study that enable graduates to be employed at major corporations. The state of Kentucky facilitated a partnership with the university and the National Science Foundation in a program that supported training teachers from the state in content knowledge, science and technology education, and the encouragement of business support (Sanoff 2006).

Beshears and Gino (2015) describe leaders as architects as they facilitate components of building consensus and developing leadership skills in others. While their work and writing is publishing in the *Harvard Business Review*, the information is applicable to education and schools, both in higher education and K–12 systems.

UNIVERSITIES AND K–12 SCHOOLS

About ten years ago many university programs in educational leadership began focusing on information provided by the business world, and organizational theory and change were merged in the disciplines. The study of best practices is supported by that collaborative work between disciplines. Educational leadership programs study the works of leaders in business because the leadership theory is applicable to the organization of schools (Barsh and Lavoie 2014; Canfield 2015; Maxwell 2013; Hewertson 2015).

Leadership concepts and skills apply to all organizations. Strong leaders can lead any organization with the consideration of the attributes as showing in Figure 1.1.

TEACHER AND EDUCATIONAL LEADERSHIP PREPARATION PROGRAMS

There are several key components embedded into a university education preparation program to enhance the learning experience of students and increase the possibility for student success (Delmont 2011). Researchers identified these components and support the recognition of variations between programs based on state accreditation, state regulations, and programs that require state or industry standards (Auerbach 2011; Baker, Pifer, and Flemion 2013; Kyvik and Olsen 2012).

The departments of education in each state drive regulatory requirements of both K–12 schools and institutes of higher education. Requirements vary by state, but all states must meet federal requirements. Every Student Succeeds Act (ESSA) is the law that replaced No Child Left Behind (NCLB, 2002) and strategic engagement and partnerships between stakeholders and organizations are a vital component of the new law. Funding may support initiatives of partnership, specifically if the gap between practitioners and policy makers is addressed, teacher leadership is facilitated, and professional

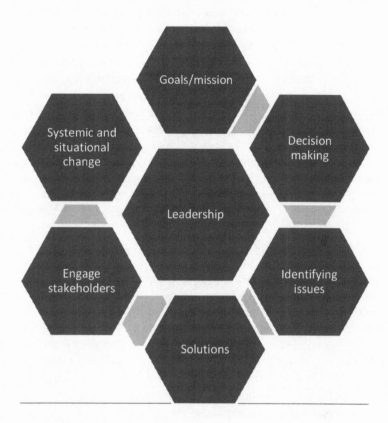

Figure 1.1. Attributes of a Good Leader

development activities provided (Fennell 2016). A university could provide the professional development training and research component as an example of a partnership entity.

As indicated in figure 1.1, attributes of partnerships should be a focus of collaborative work. Partnerships between regional school districts and teacher preparatory programs are important to insure that student learning standards are embedded in course content of the university programs. Practitioners use data to drive instructional changes in K–12 settings to improve student outcomes. Similarly, teacher training programs need to be accountable, using data to align course content, field work experiences, and feedback to students to improve teacher practice.

Collaborative efforts between schools, school districts, and teacher preparatory programs provide benefits to all stakeholders (Obrien 2014). Teacher quality and student performance improves when shared competencies are communicated and focused upon. Many researchers have provided insights to partnerships between school, and institutes of higher education (IHE) in regards to teacher preparation programs (Ammentorp and Madden 2014; Layton 2014; Rosenberg et al. 2009; Petersen 2014; Wallace 2009).

High quality partnerships between schools and universities are developing programs to close the gap between research, preparation, and practice. Practitioners identify gaps in new teachers that inform programs and when universities have a system in place to respond and change courses to better meet the needs of districts, teacher prep programs provide a needed resource for schools.

The importance of partnerships and the impact of successful partnership development will guide the changes now required in ESSA. Many states have created rules and regulations, prior to ESSA, that specifically require partnerships between K–12 schools and university programs that engage and develop leaders. In Missouri, a law was passed in 2013 that provided funding for educational partnerships between higher education institutions, businesses, and K–12 schools; in Virginia, a 2010 law was passed that allowed universities that operate a teacher prep program to operate and work together with local districts to host K–12 schools; in Idaho, a law was adopted in 2008 to support K–12 and university partnerships; in Indiana, a 2007 law was passed that authorized four universities to establish and support K–12 schools by allowing them to enter into a contract with the local school districts in Indiana to support teaching, learning, and student outcomes; and in Hawaii, a 2013 law was passed creating a partnership between a university and after school program support for children in need of additional academic support (Education Commission of the States Policy, 2016). These are just a few examples of how university partnerships can impact K–12 faculty, businesses, community agencies, and programs of study in higher education.

A task force made up of faculty, administrators, alumni, graduates, and community members is an effective way to facilitate input from stakeholders. Meeting a few times a year provides communication and collaborative opportunities that inform practice.

Changes that might occur as a result of stakeholder communication could be an increase in field work; realignment of goals and learning outcomes; additional coursework in specific areas, such as classroom management or communicating effectively with parents. Feedback to university program faculty from practitioners is critical to inform a partnership and sharing of successes and challenges. Program alignment with practitioner needs support changes in curriculum, course alignment, and shared goals for graduates of programs.

The Yale–New Haven Teachers Institute has facilitated increasing teacher's skills through school–university partnerships (Fry 2015). Focus on increased content knowledge, active learning strategies, and alignment with standards and best practices of instruction are the subjects of multiple seminars provided by university faculty to teachers through the institute's program of professional development. This enables a stronger teacher preparation program of studies and supports a partnership initiative of increased collaboration.

Collaboration in field placement experience can truly support pre-service teachers and administrators (Ammentorp and Madden 2014). Teaching and learning is a collaborative process, and when university students have increased opportunities to be in field placements, working with teachers, the real life experience supports classroom instruction and ultimate goals of students.

COLLABORATION

Collaboration is a key aspect of successful partnerships between organizations (Wasonga, Rari, and Wanzare 2011). These authors identified a comprehensive process of acknowledgment that establishing shared goals and values toward partnership goals is complex. They identified mentoring programs, professional development, research, pre-service programs (internships, field placements), and job placement as significant components of collaborative projects.

Collaborative processes require partners to implement four concepts well: planning, decision-making, implementation, and evaluating outcomes (Gardner 2011). Evaluators from Illinois State University researched characteristics in school-university partnerships. They identified that the intent of partnerships is greatly supported, but actualizing the intended purpose can be a challenge. Policy strategies of partnerships do not always coincide well with practitioner beliefs and desires.

Jones et al. (2012) described how distributive leadership can serve as the framework for collaboration between institutes of higher education, businesses, and K–12 school system leaders. They define collective collaboration as an approach that placed emphasis on team decision making and responsibility, rather than the power and control of individual leaders. The result of their study indicated that shared leadership is a skill that leaders need to support partnerships successfully. Leadership capacity was strengthened by this distributive leadership approach and impacted all in learning and teaching.

Pisano and Verganti (2013) identified collaboration in businesses and how to think about leveraging types of collaboration that would be beneficial for various corporations. The pros and cons of the four models they described are applicable to all disciplines, and support that, while differences within organizations may help drive decisions, leadership can benefit from consideration of collaborative plans.

Global leadership competencies for various educational positions have been identified in various studies (Goodman 2012; Litz 2011; Terrell 2011; Sullivan 2011). Key competencies included vision, integrity, content knowledge, confidence, decision making, an understanding of organizational systems, problem solving, operational management, and commitment. These competencies apply to all organizations, based on theories and research across disciplines.

KEY IDEAS IN THIS CHAPTER

- Partnerships matter at universities and K–12 schools
- Collaboration is a key to success
- Leadership skills are not limited to one discipline
- Leadership can be developed
- Values-based leadership supports all organizations

SUMMARY

Building leadership capacity is strengthened through various partnerships in all fields. University, community, and K–12 schools afford partnership opportunities that strengthen programs, create leadership paths for sustainability and programs of succession in businesses, schools, agencies, and universities. Leadership transcends across cultures, and as reported in Idea Watch (*Harvard Business Review*, May 2015), in various countries across the globe, building and sustaining relationships, increasing your team's capacity, recognizing the values and structures of organizations, focusing on goal and mission alignment and purpose are critical aspects of leadership development.

Chapter Two

University Partnerships

Fern Aefsky, Susan Kinsella, Lorrie McGovern, and Christine Sereni-Massinger

Successful partnerships are defined by their organizational structure (Wasonga, Rari, and Wanzare 2011). Shared goals, vision, and missions, beneficial to all partners, agreement for collaboration, commitment, and resource support are the basis for collaborative partnerships.

University leadership has significant issues to continuously consider, including the rising costs of higher education, student retention rates, and graduation rates (Burdman 2008; Marcus 2008; Noland 2011; Zemsky and Finney 2010). Policies, mandates, and regulations differ by state, but the requirements of standards for institutions of higher education are often not recognized by practitioners in business, education, or community service agencies.

Developing partnerships has enabled universities globally to build capacity of others in order to improve relationships that foster solutions through innovation and program delivery, improving retention, graduation rates, and a needed link between practitioners and program development in higher education (Jones et al. 2012).

They identified a leadership approach that embraces collaboration and creating a collaborative framework for university practitioners with business executives and professionals that support graduating students with effective leadership capabilities. Their study was conducted at four universities in Australia and provided aspects of sustainable leadership at the university level that enabled partnership success.

Community partnerships have been developed as part of integrated programs at many universities. Northern Kentucky University has focused their energy on building links with the surrounding community in order to enhance growth in the geographical region (Marcus 2008). Engaging the community was a part of the economic planning process developed in the community in collaboration with the business development team in the area.

In California, the Western Interstate Commission for Higher Education identified challenges that require policy change and implementation (Burdman 2008). In collaboration with the California EDGE campaign (Education, Diversity and Growth in the Economy), focus on how institutes of higher education could graduate leaders in various industries that would drive policy development that supported students, communities, and practitioners' needs in the fields of education and business.

In West Virginia, an initiative was begun to enable institutes of higher education to drive programs of innovation and economic development (Noland 2011). This program was built upon partnerships with civic, corporate, and community partnerships and a partnership with legislative leadership to enable policy development to support the initiative. This initiative was critical in identifying that higher education was an important factor in developing human capital and that partnerships with constituents matter in the creation of policy to support those partnerships and the emerging leaders from university programs.

These are just a few examples of universities that identified partnerships as important entities for policy, program, student, and practitioner needs. Through partnerships, leadership capacity is nurtured and practiced.

LEADERSHIP DEVELOPMENT

Distributed leadership in Institutes of Higher Education (IHE) has been identified as a new challenge for global consideration (Jones et al. 2014). In order to build leadership capacity and embrace collaboration by engaging stakeholders, these authors studied Australian higher education institutes and institutional practices of interdependencies impacting leadership practices. Active participation to support institutional growth and change led to the development of a national leadership program initiative, the Leadership for Excellence in Learning and Teaching Program (ALTC, 2009). The resulting framework supported collaborative opportunities, with resources, to enable stakeholders to develop innovative practices and leadership distribution.

COLLABORATION

The following pages provide examples of successful partnerships that help build the capacity of effective leaders through intra- and interuniversity collaboration. University programs of studies are engaging in more collaborative initiatives than ever before. Multiple areas and departments are involved in partnerships that help leaders develop skills and programs graduate students with skills to be successive leaders. Teacher and school administrator preparatory programs are an important, but not the only university program of study that supports collaborative leadership development.

HUMAN SERVICES PROGRAM AND PARTNERSHIPS

Teaching students how to build relationships with community partners is a necessary skill in both undergraduate and graduate human services programs (Ouellette, Briscoe, and Tyson 2004). This practice helps students develop leadership skills through practice in their field.

Human services and business students have worked with social service professionals as they interned with non-profit agencies and learned about Board of Trustee governance, development of leadership skills, and an understanding of the value of community service (Purdy and Lawless 2012). In their study, a course in Board Governance was included with an internship at a non-profit organization to create a service-learning activity for students. In this way students learned about community needs, social responsibility, and collaboration with other disciplines. Universities, students, and community agencies all benefited because students recognized the value of service and leadership.

Several studies have focused on the outcomes of interdisciplinary practice. In an effort to prepare Human Services students for this type of interdisciplinary work, one study focused on a training model. It introduced graduate students from clinical psychology, social work, education, and physical therapy to a practice setting where they could collaborate using the expertise from their profession. Results indicated that students who participated in this training had a higher level of learning regarding their knowledge and practice (Knauss et al. 2003).

It has become increasingly difficult for just one helping profession to meet the needs of clients who often have multiple issues. Specialized skill sets from one discipline can connect quite nicely with another discipline, offering a variety of options for the client and the social service agency to explore. The outcome can be a solution with various services, interventions, and resources for the individual, group, or family. In a university setting, this means that faculty are beginning to collaborate with other disciplines to create a framework that will shape the thinking and practice of students.

Human Services is defined as a multidisciplinary study of processes to facilitate client determined systematic change at all levels of society (Kincaid 2009). In order to do this, the curriculum is designed to reflect various perspectives and courses from such fields as psychology, sociology, social work, criminal justice, as well as human services.

Over time many studies have continually shown a beneficial link between such disciplines as social work and education as student interns in both disciplines have worked within a school setting in collaboration with a school social worker (Lopez, Torres, and Norwood 1998). In another study of inner city schools, parents, teachers, and human services workers engaged in a partnership for at-risk youth and their families. Some networking strategies were successful, although communication challenges did exist. In other studies between education and human services partnerships, collaborative efforts were aimed at providing services to school children and their families in response to children's health issues.

School districts often integrate public health and social services into the school system (Caruso 2000). As a result of these initiatives, universities should be considering courses that blend the learning of social services, health, and communication. Classes that include service projects that involve students in school settings or in projects that teach students how to identify and provide necessary health services to high risk children and their families should be considered.

In their book *Collaborative Practice, School and Human Service Partnerships* (1999) Jean Mooney and Robbie Tourse examined the need for necessary partnerships between schools and human service agencies. If social issues are to be resolved, then a team of interdisciplinary professionals is needed to work with children and their families in the schools. Issues such as poverty, homelessness, developmental disabilities, family violence, and substance abuse are just a few of the many problems facing our schools and communities. Interventions based upon identification and diagnosis of learning disabilities, resource and referral for social services, parent education, counseling, and rehabilitation services all require a coordinated team effort. This makes collaboration within a university a priority and the use of intra- and interconnecting departments favorable.

By working within the universities to build partnerships through interconnecting departments, faculty have the opportunity to enhance student learning. The knowledge, values, and skills learned by students can then be transferred to practice through community linking teaching strategies (MacTavish et al. 2006). For instance, courses that include education projects and grant-writing partnerships in community agencies, offer students the opportunity to put knowledge learned in the classroom into practice. This amalgamation of learning is useful for the new practitioner who needs to identify and access resources, work within social service networks, and build partnerships with professionals from other disciplines. This is necessary if they are to be successful advocates for their clients.

Partnerships between universities and communities can also lend strength to the learning process. In one study of service learning projects at two universities, human services students and social work students were offered the opportunity to link theory to practice by working with immigrant and minority families in transitional neighborhoods (Brown and Kinsella 2006). In one project, a neighborhood family support center was established in a disadvantaged neighborhood by a collaboration of university departments. Residents of African American, Latino, or Anglo backgrounds shared a community resource center that provided English classes, day care, parenting classes, legal assistance, case management, needs assessments, counseling, as well as social activities for the children and adults in an attempt to develop a cohesive neighborhood.

Graduate and undergraduate students from a variety of disciplines with expertise in social work, architecture, political science, sociology, psychology, business, landscape engineering, law, and education worked with residents to assist with the creation of the center, complete the garden and outdoor landscaping, design and build a playground for the children, teach in the after-school day care, and offer English classes and translation services for the immigrant families who lived nearby.

Services like family budgeting, tax preparation, banking, as well as legal counseling for citizenship were crucial. Successful outcomes for the residents were realized with a decrease in crime due to a more engaged and aware community with plenty of parental involvement. The influence of local gangs was diminished since parent, community, and university collaboration was strong.

University students benefited by learning about community development models, creating and building a center and outdoor playground area, practicing advocacy, counseling on legal issues, developing cultural diversity curricula to be used in the community center, teaching residents and their children, facilitating a variety of groups, and using business accounting techniques with the residents such as tax preparation, budgeting, and household finance.

A second project at another institution also involved a partnership with the university and several rural counties surrounding the school. Basic services were seen as necessary for a quickly increasing Latino population due to agricultural needs. A Latino outreach center was developed with the goal of the partnership between the center and the university to increase integration of the Latino population. Since the families did not speak English, academic and social supports were needed for the children to participate in school. The Center for Latino Outreach and Research Services was developed and included faculty from such disciplines as political science, sociology, social services, business, education, language arts, nursing, and dental hygiene.

Student learning outcomes included increased knowledge of cultural diversity, community problem assessment and resolution, advocacy, case management, interviewing, research, increased use and knowledge of Spanish, increased empathy, and knowledge regarding social and legal issues.

These two projects employed faculty who created partnerships within their departments as well as with other departments within their universities to allow for collaboration with their local community agencies. Together they prepared students to work with crisis oriented and low-income neighborhoods near their universities. Results indicated a plethora of new services for clients as a result of service learning and field placement opportunities created by faculty and students. Outcomes of the two projects also indicated that better communication and support among neighbors was high.

Successes also included new and accessible services for a growing immigrant population. Development, implementation, and maintenance of the partnerships in the two locations required faculty to balance their traditional academic roles with those in the community. Student learning was perceived as high with invaluable practice opportunities.

In a current undergraduate program for Human Services at Saint Leo University, students complete service learning projects or volunteer at an agency in each course. They practice skills they have learned in the classroom by assisting agencies with a fundraising activity or grant, facilitate a group for a children's center, collect resources for a homeless shelter, or assist with resource and referral at a local agency.

In addition, partnerships are created with local agencies for more academic field placements where students complete at least 350 hours of supervised work. Faculty monitor the field placement settings and act as liaisons between the university and agency setting, ensuring that students are completing required educational goals. In addition to daily work, students complete reflective journals and maintain weekly contact with their university liaison through e-mail communication and periodic seminars.

Agency supervisors evaluate students based upon written criteria provided by the university. Students earn academic credit for the work completed. These partnerships with the agencies are critical to the successful learning outcomes for human services students. Administrators of these programs also serve on a Human Services Community Advisory Board that meets quarterly at the university. Their role in the Human Services program is to inform the department of ongoing community needs, changes to services, requirements for students, and employment opportunities.

The need for more intra- and interdepartmental collaboration within universities is evident. As faculty develop inter- and intradepartmental teams to work on cross-discipline projects, there are benefits to students as well as the university. In a recent study bbroad trip to Denmark, Saint Leo University faculty from business, education, social work, and human services and graduate business students coordinated efforts in visiting several social service agencies in cities across their country.

Observations and discussions among faculty and students were paired with meetings of professionals from social services agencies in Denmark to discuss such issues as political and social philosophies of social welfare, social policies, taxes, health care, family issues, aging, earned income, and business principles. Since Denmark was in the midst of their annual National Reform, it was particularly relevant to discuss these issues and to think critically about them from several different perspectives.

This type of dialogue is dynamic since it involves an analysis of frameworks from various disciplines resulting in a broader understanding of the topic. Positive outcomes for both faculty and students were shared and a continued collaboration across disciplines will continue with other trips and projects.

The scholarship of engaging students in the learning process has become very important within university settings (Calvert 2011). The development of a multi- or interdisciplinary approach has gained momentum since it teaches students, in a broad sense, collaboration with other disciplines as well as a sense of social responsibilities, leadership, ethical issues, and values.

As an interdisciplinary profession, this is very evident in Human Services. The collaboration of university departments along with the development of university and community partnerships has proven that internships, service learning, and coordinated community projects, all key concepts in human services training, allows students to link theory to practice. When universities and communities work together faculty and students gain valuable practice experience.

Students who receive education in universities that prepare them to work in a variety of social service settings with a multidisciplinary team of professionals will be better prepared to deal with the multiple and critical needs of clients. As a result, faculty need to be creative in their approach to course development and preparation. Including other social science, business, and health disciplines into the discussion of student training should be encouraged in an effort to increase the knowledge base of human services students.

CRIMINAL JUSTICE PROGRAM AND PARTNERSHIPS

Introduction

Educational institutions partner with law enforcement agencies to provide annual certification training on subject matter issues such as: constitutional law, criminal procedure, courtroom procedure, and civil liability. Few agencies request and, therefore, few educational institutions provide, agencies' training in critical thinking. Offering free annual certification training courses geared to cross-cultural critical thinking can assist both the agencies and the communities they serve in building trust and mending current community factions.

Educational opportunities geared to critical thinking have spawned attitudinal changes in major community issues such as civil rights, politics, authoritarianism, and leadership by encouraging examination of personal biases and assumptions (Hess and Orthmann 2012). Critical thinking training for law enforcement officers can enhance their ability to lead in diverse communities by building solid relationships and trust (Roberg, Novak, and Cordner 2005).

LEADERSHIP DEVELOPMENT

Leaders in areas of criminal justice (police authorities, cybersecurity, homeland security) face challenges of the specifics of the job and community reaction to those in the jobs described above. Stiehm (2014) discussed the fact that more management tasks than leadership strategies occur during tough times. The need to get things done, rather than lead the way for others to assist in getting things done becomes a challenge when reactions to situations occur.

For example, the public reaction to police shootings in urban areas, where white policemen and women have shot African American men has created reactive, managerial tasks of maintaining peace and safety. However, in these situations leadership skills of stakeholders is critical, from police agencies, community leaders, and all stakeholders.

Researchers have identified the need for leaders to establish organizational missions, vision, and values (Llopis 2014; Stiehm 2014). Organizational leadership characteristics in criminal justice are synonymous with leadership qualities identified in other areas of study.

COLLABORATION

The Criminal Justice Department at Saint Leo University has been instrumental in providing certification training to law enforcement agents across the United States. Certification training assists agents in continued education after their initial date of hire. Agencies such as sheriff's offices, police departments, corrections and prosecutors' offices have promoted and encouraged their agents to attend seminars offered by Saint Leo University for annual certification training.

In the last several years Saint Leo University has partnered with these agencies in the following annual certification trainings:

- Testifying Made Easy
- Criminal Justice Ethics
- The Prosecution of Ted Bundy
- Interrogation Techniques
- 4th, 5th, and 6th Amendment Supreme Court Rulings
- Stand Your Ground Law
- Human Trafficking
- Investigation and Prosecution Techniques
- Threat Assessment of a Loan Shooter
- Crime Mapping
- Conflict Resolution

Presenters from Saint Leo University are trained to guide law enforcement attendees in self–regulation, problem-solving, and critical thinking skills. Thus, agencies that partner with higher educational institutions such as Saint Leo greatly benefit by not only receiving the content of the seminar, but also in receiving the content in a manner that promotes improved professional decision making.

As a result of the increase in negative opinions toward law enforcement, expansion of Community Oriented Policing (COP) is now needed to include partnering with educational institutions on critical thinking training. Critical thinking instruction should begin in the academy and continue through annual certification training until an officer's retirement. Training in cross-cultural competence should be provided to officers prior to their initial outreach within their communities.

By applying critical thinking, agencies can learn how to more effectively approach citizens in cross-cultural communities. Factions between police and the communities they serve could potentially lessen. Critical thinking is a skill necessary in law enforcement because of the high stress and unpredictable nature of the profession. Instruction in cross-cultural leadership through critical thinking can assist officers in finding multiple solutions to the encounters that they face daily within their diverse communities.

Advancements have been made in fostering community partnerships with the implementation of COP. Criminal justice agencies that form effective community partnerships serve to: decrease crime, resolve community conflict, and educate agency personnel. With multiculturalism at the heart of our American society, a law enforcement officer's oath increasingly requires the effective interaction with, and leadership of, citizens from diverse backgrounds. Agencies can enhance their ability to effectively relate to all citizens by forming partnerships with educational institutions that train on cross-cultural leadership through the application of critical thinking.

COP has been a relatively effective approach to building relationships between law enforcement agencies and the communities that they serve

(Wehrman and DeAngelis 2011). However, with community opinions toward law enforcement officers negatively changing, an expansion of COP is now necessary (Hudson 2014).

The growing multicultural population in the United States is creating greater challenges for law enforcement officers to effectively relate to the diverse members of their communities (Williams 2012). This chapter addresses how negative community opinions toward police can be minimized when law enforcement agencies partner with educational institutions to include training in cross-cultural leadership on critical thinking application. Traditional, substantive training is not enough (Vodde 2009).

In the criminal justice realm, critical thinking training is instrumental in developing multiple solutions to the problems officers routinely encounter by training officers to challenge their assumptions and biases. This training can be relevant in improving officers' decision-making processes leading to beneficial community and agency outcomes (Safi and Burell 2007).

COP has gained popularity. Formations of partnerships with the community have been a valuable asset for criminal justice agencies (Skogan et al. 2002). Studies show that COP serves to increase public support and to build trust since officers strive to consistently meet with community stakeholders on a routine basis (Diamond and Weiss 2009). Since 1995, more than 90 percent of police agencies serving populations over 25,000 have adopted the COP method (Morabito 2010).

As part of the COP model, many agencies have invested time and effort in forming partnerships with minority residents in an effort to build trust and confidence (Wehrman and DeAngelis 2011). Part of building trust and being an effective leader in the criminal justice field involves an ability to be culturally competent (Hudson 2014).

Researchers posit the more information that diverse citizens are willing to share with police, the safer their environment becomes (Wells et al. 2006). Research also shows that awareness of cultural differences within the community is an important aspect of crime prevention and problem-solving (Payne and Button 2009). This open communication and ongoing engagement between community members and the police positively impacts the safety of the community and builds trust with the community partners (Connell, Miggans, and McGloin 2008).

With the growing multicultural nature of communities, COP must evolve to include a comprehensive educational plan with higher education institutions capable of providing training in problem-solving skills geared to critical thinking (Connell, Miggons, and McGlan 2008). Critical thinking is a readily applicable skill in the majority of professions and can create greater gains in a professional's ability to analyze, approach, and solve problems (Bensley 2010). Critical thinking has been defined as: "1) identifying the assumptions that frame our thinking and determine our actions 2) checking out the degree to which these assumptions are accurate and valid 3) looking at our ideas and decisions from several different perspectives 4) on the basis of this, making informed decisions" (Brookfield 2011).

Although many agencies partner with educational institutions in traditional training, few partner with these institutions in critical thinking training geared to cross-cultural competence. Research indicates that a positive relationship exists between enhancement of law enforcement performance and critical thinking training including: problem-solving, effective decision making, and the ability to communicate with and relate to individuals from diverse backgrounds (Breci 1994; Smith and Aamodt 1997; Hardwick Day 2002).

COP has been historically a relatively effective approach to decreasing crime, resolving community conflict, and assisting in educational training for law enforcement personnel (Diamond and Weiss 2009). According to this model, the community takes an active role and works collaboratively with police agencies to reduce crime. Community members are given personal responsibility to their community and become an integral part of maintaining order (Morabito 2010).

Communication and trust is encouraged through this method. As neighbors watch out for neighbors the model's emphasis is placed on social cohesion and collective efficacy. Several impactful programs were generated as a result of the COP method. These programs are still viable in many communities throughout the United States today including: neighborhood watches, citizens' patrols, and other such programs (Taylor 2002; Xu, Fiedler, and Flaming 2005).

In the last several years, COP has attempted to address the resolution of community conflict by creating a one-on-one approach through the formation of personal relationships leading to solid community connections. Law enforcement officers are given long-term assignments based on the area of the community in which they live. Officers strive to establish ongoing connections and relationships with the members of that community through a series of consistent interactions (Chappell 2009, p. 12).

Agencies encourage officers to maintain contact and relationships with the members of their communities even when they are off duty (Connell, Miggins, and McGlan 2008, p. 133). The increase in police visibility, whether through patrol or less formal interactions such as visits to stores and homes, serves to reduce fear and enhances public opinion of the police (Dalgleish and Myhill 2004). It is the establishment of geographic accountability and the increase in familiarity between community residents and their officers that have had a positive effect on the reduction of community conflict (Diamond and Weiss 2009).

Officers who have a working relationship with the community members who they protect and serve feel a degree of responsibility toward them. With the one-on-one and relationship-building approach, police-citizen interactions become more personal and less formal and cultural differences lessen (Connell, Miggans, and McGloin 2008).

Further enhancement of the COP method is now needed (Hudson 2014). Such growth can take place if officers are trained to think critically about their diverse communities before they attempt to establish relationships in those communities. Partnering with educational institutions that train in cross-cultural leadership through critical thinking can assist both law enforcement personnel and the communities that they serve.

Studies reveal that the formation of police community partnerships with educational institutions can further build trust in the community (Morabito 2010). Formation of partnerships between law enforcement agencies and educational institutions is essential toward resolving conflict by training officers to critically examine the key issues that are the root causes of these conflicts. Police officers who understand the diverse members of their community are more inclined to create effective relationships with them.

When law enforcement prioritizes community partnerships, cultural divides lessen and safer environments can be created (Chappell 2009). Training in social intelligence and understanding of diversity is a key aspect of an officer's effectiveness within that community and the training should occur early in the officer's career and continue annually until the officer's retirement (Williams 2012).

Police-related civil disturbances have resulted in finding ways to connect with communities to overcome distrust and is imperative. Policing is certainly unpredictable and volatile. Officers are met some days with mundane tasks and other days with life threatening situations.

It is for these reasons that a balanced approach to law enforcement training and education is necessary. Training and education should be focused not only on the daily responsibilities to the community but also on situational awareness and understanding of the diverse community members (Vodde 2009).

Very few agencies mandate their officers to have higher education (Pace 2000). Recent research reveals that less than 1 percent of all law enforcement agencies in the United States have a four-year degree requirement (Hickman and Reaves 2006). Furthermore, many officers enter into the profession through the successful completion of the police academy that is historically paramilitary in approach (Vodde 2009).

In many of these academies traditional and more substantive training is offered. In the state of Florida, for example, the Florida Basic Recruit Training Program textbook has several pages dedicated to diversity. However, the content of these pages is more substantively based (that is, defining the various members of the community who comprise a diverse society) (Florida Department of Law Enforcement 2014).

It would be the discretion of the individual instructor to incorporate critical thinking skills regarding this topic. Currently, in the Florida Basic Recruit Training Program textbook, there are no individual chapters dedicated to applying critical thinking skills to relate to diverse community members (Florida Department of Law Enforcement 2014). There are also no courses offered that are based on critical thinking as a topic in and of itself.

Researchers posit that training in areas of ethics, integrity, and discretion should begin at the academy and follow an officer until retirement (Diamond and Weiss 2009). Officers should receive academy training on critical thinking as well as receive continued annual certification training to include "exercises for the formation and maintenance of good habits and character, as well as exercises in value choices, ethical dilemmas, and discretion in police work" (Delattre 2006, 52). Real-world exercises in choices and decision-making are an integral aspect of critical thinking (Brookfield 2011; Paul and Elder 2010).

Studies show the traditional, military model of police training is ineffective compared to an andragogical model that focuses on teaching adult problem solving skills through critical thinking (Vodde 2009; Safi and Burell 2007). According to Knowles' theory of andragogy, adults are self-directed and will take responsibility for their learning. Knowles opined that adult instruction should be more focused on the process of problem solving and less focused on the actual materials or content being presented (Knowles, Swanson, and Holton 2005).

Providing instruction in officer training that applies critical thinking strategies encourages focus on problem solving and is more appropriate for adult learning. Traditional police training has focused more on the "how" whereas critical thinking police training focuses more on the "why" (Vodde 2009).

The current COP model has cited a consistent element of their approach to include, "Using problem-oriented or problem-solving approaches involving police personnel working with community members" (*Protecting Civil Rights* 2006). Problem solving is linked to critical thinking (Brookfield 2011). Critical thinking police training allows for a greater understanding on the part of the officers of the diverse communities that they serve (Roberg, Kuykendall, and Novak 2002).

Since policing requires structure and discipline at the organizational level as well as on the personal level, researchers posit that to effectively change communities where cultural divides is an issue, a less bureaucratic approach needs to be developed (Roberg, Novak, and Cordner 2005). A more philosophical approach to training can be achieved with the standardized incorporation of critical thinking into current instruction (Brookfield 2011).

Offering courses based solely on critical thinking skills would also be of benefit. Traditional training is currently ineffective (Vodde 2009; Diamond and Weiss 2009). The challenges faced by today's COP require enhancement of instruction to include education in critical thinking, advanced problem solving skills, and interpersonal skills (Kappeler and Gaines 2005). Since police officers are required to make critical decisions in some of the most traumatic circumstances, higher-level learning and critical thinking skills are necessary (Carlan and Byxbe 2000).

SCHOOL OF BUSINESS

Introduction

There are different types of program initiatives that support collaboration and partnerships in the school of business. Between disciplines within the school and with other schools and the community, partnerships have created opportunities for students and faculty to support collaboration and leadership. All stakeholders must be involved for successful partnerships, collaborative projects, and leadership development.

The primary stakeholders are our students, parents, administration, Board of Trustees, alumni, donors, community leaders, faculty, staff, and our business and military partners. A holistic approach to academic excellence in higher education involves more than just interaction between the students and faculty. An effective school of business within a university needs to actively engage community partners to successfully achieve its ultimate goal of educating students in preparation for successful careers. Community partners are external stakeholders while the students, staff, and faculty are internal stakeholders.

Freeman (1984, p. 16) defines a stakeholder as "any group or individual who can affect or is affected by the achievement of the firm's objectives." Due to the impact these stakeholders have on the organization, Freeman suggests that organizations need to develop a relationship with the stakeholders and consider their perspective when developing the organization's strategic plans. This business approach to achieving a firm's objectives transcends industry and is consistent with achieving a university's objectives.

The original 1984 stakeholder model proposed by Freeman shows the firm at the center with representatives that are both internal and external to the firm (Fassin 2009, p. 11, figure 2.1). Between 1984 until 2003, Freeman's model evolved, as illustrated in Figure 2.2 (Fassin 2009, p. 11).

In 2008, Jongbloed described how Freeman's stakeholder model was applicable to higher education. He stated, "In higher education, the most important, or core, community would be the students" (Jongbloed, Enders, and Salano 2008, 305). In public education, the government is the main funder and thereby a significant stakeholder; however, within a non-profit setting, the government does not provide this resource.

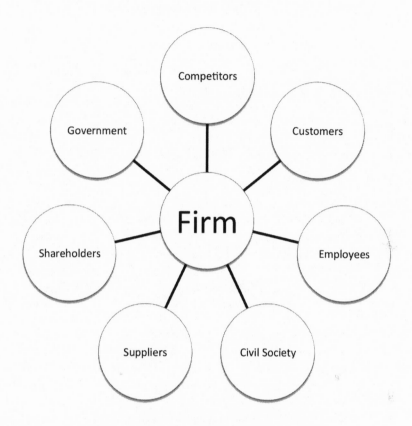

Figure 2.1. The Original Stakeholder Model—Freeman (1984)

LEADERSHIP DEVELOPMENT

The engagement of community partners is extremely important in the university's quest for academic excellence. As with any valuable long-term relationship, everyone needs to receive some type of benefit from the relationship.

Participants in collaborative partnerships gain leadership skills through various activities. Students benefit from the relationship between the university and community partners by securing experiential learning opportunities and meeting with valuable business contacts. Student interaction with the community partners can take a variety of different forms. Students could merely network with them at events or meetings, or the students could gain an opportunity for a mentorship or internship experience which can help them learn more about a specific employer and help them apply the knowledge learned in the classroom at the workplace. In addition to the site supervisor at an internship, students have a chance to engage with other employees

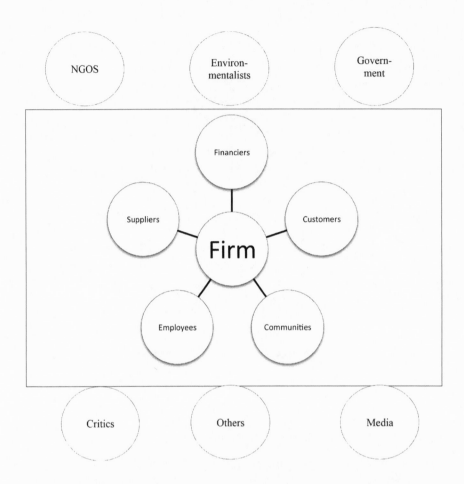

Figure 2.2. The adapted version of the stakeholder model—Freeman (2003)

of the organization and this helps them develop their professional and leadership skills.

There are many opportunities through schools of business to develop leaders. In one university, the marketing department is engaged with a local boys and girls club in an area where there are significant issues of poverty. The children attend an elementary school where there is a free and reduced lunch rate of 100 percent, and students from migrant families and the local community represent a +95 percent African American and Latino population.

The students from the boys and girls club come to the campus twice a month for dinner and presentations and activities from across the school. Students at the university volunteer to assist, and faculty present information and activities that engage students, motivate an interest in pursuing college and career goals, and faculty engage in presenting workshops for these students in grades K–12.

The American Marketing Association (AMA) sponsors these events, as college students in the marketing program volunteer. The university students develop marketing plans and programs that engage the students in the boys and girls club, and within this partnership all benefit. The AMA activity may involve university students having the elementary students make cards, then the marketing students develop a plan to sell the cards and donate the monies raised to the club or a service project of the club.

This is one example of how students develop leadership skills, following the leaders in the school of business that benefits the community through a partnership program.

The community partner benefits by having a relationship with the organization developing the talent pool. They have the opportunity to influence the curriculum and gain early access to the students prior to graduation. Most students need internships and this is an ideal method of screening for employers and employees.

The benefits to the university include feedback on curriculum to ensure students learn the competencies required to launch successful careers. The career success of the student is linked to the overall success of the business degree programs at the university. Students need to feel as though they are prepared to launch a career upon graduation from a program. Successful graduates are more generous alumni, and this all plays into the organizational benefits for the university.

Relationships with community partners can also benefit the university financially through scholarships or tuition reimbursement awarded to employees who may attend the university. In addition, the university could benefit from other philanthropy opportunities offered by the community partners.

Over the past seven years, the Donald R. Tapia School of Business at Saint Leo University has focused on developing a stronger community partnership with industry. This success has been achieved through development of industry councils that create a collaborative working relation between the organizations and the university. The strategic plan documents the commitment made by the business school to these primary stakeholders.

1. Demonstrate academic excellence where student competencies meet the needs of business, including applying our core values; the ability to think critically; use technology and analytics to improve decision making; and commit to professional development for life.
2. Create and deliver programs that remain loyal to the mission, vision, values, and needs of the institution and business.

3. Establish a community where our core values are demonstrated by students, faculty, and staff through open communication and mutual respect in our interactions and in our participation in service to the larger community beyond Saint Leo.
4. Communicate goals, strategies, and expectations that support (financially and intrinsically) our efforts including individual accountability.
5. Build a leadership team including all levels of management, faculty, and staff that are capable and committed to implementing the school's vision and mission and sustaining that leadership for future generations (Donald 2012, p. 2).

The business school works closely with many community business partners. Examples include working with Pasco Economic Development Council (PEDC), Tampa Economic Development Council (TBEC), and the Tampa Bay Task Force on Technology. In keeping with our core values and Benedictine traditions of community involvement, Saint Leo has been a contributing member of these forums for a number of years.

Practitioners involved in blending content knowledge with practicum experiences as part of applied research in doctoral level coursework are able to use experiences in their workplace to contributing to the related work in a global economy. Research supports the implication for applied dissertations in various fields, but recognizes variations between programs based on state accreditation, state regulations, programs that require state or industry standards (Auerbach 2011; Baker, Pifer, and Flemion 2013; Kyvik and Olsen 2012).

Doctoral degrees designed for the continuing education of professionals are part of the global perspectives of diversity and expansion of practitioners' work in business and education. A collaborative approach of shared competencies strengthens programs. In the global economy, the relationships between schools and businesses are significant. For example, the national targets in Europe, Europe 2020, include five targets: (1) employment; (2) research and development; (3) climate and energy; (4) education; and (5) social inclusion. Each component includes an educational and business goal and standard (European Commission, 2014). Furthermore, the National Reform Programme in Denmark (2014) incorporates unique initiatives for Denmark in 2013 in addition to the National Targets in Europe 2020.

The Doctorate in Business Administration (DBA) is an advanced degree program that prepares graduates with research, critical analysis, and application skills to make an intellectual contribution to their field of business study. Saint Leo University's DBA program builds on its values that emphasize social responsibility, innovation, and accountability to foster a new form of leadership focused on creating vibrant and sustainable organizations. Students gain an in-depth understanding of the functional business areas, practical skills for leading within an organization, and methods for shaping responsible leaders.

TEACHER PREPARATORY PROGRAMS

Introduction

In 2012, U.S. Education Secretary, Arne Duncan, proposed regulations that would require each state to issue report cards for all teacher preparation programs at private and public universities that rated each program in four areas based on how teacher candidates performed after graduation (Layton 2014). The rating variables included: if the teachers get jobs in their subject field; how long they stay in those jobs; and how their students perform on standardized tests measuring academic achievement. The National Council for the Accreditation of Teacher Education Programs (NCATE) anticipated the increased accountability of teacher preparation programs, linking the performance of teacher candidates and completers to student outcomes (Harris et al. 2000).

COLLABORATION

Partnerships between regional school districts and teacher preparatory programs are important to insure that student learning standards are embedded in course content of the university programs. Practitioners use data to drive instructional changes in K–12 settings to improve student outcomes. Similarly, teacher training programs need to be accountable using data to align course content, field work experiences, and feedback to students to improve teacher practice. Collaborative efforts between schools, school districts, and teacher preparatory programs provide benefits to all stakeholders (Obrien 2014). Teacher quality and student performance improves when shared competencies are communicated and focused upon.

Critical aspects in supporting accountability related to student outcomes in K–12 settings and teacher preparation programs are well documented in research. Researchers have identified the importance of connections between instructional practice and teacher preparation program components (Amrein-Beardsley, Barnett, and Ganesh 2013; Harris et al. 2000; Sawchuck 2015; Wilson 2014). The alignment between core standards, program coursework, and field experiences is extremely important in developing assessment of teacher preparation programs and student learning accountability measures.

Core standards embedded in course content, state standards for effective teacher practice, field work experience and observation of those field work experiences link the importance of reflection and action that support teachers and students in the production of positive learning objectives and goals. Feedback to students in a variety of ways supports the growth of teachers' skills, impacts data collection and analysis, and further supports the goals of increased accountability.

Requirements of teacher preparatory programs offered by universities in each state must meet that state's certification requirements. Those requirements are linked to each state's standards for teacher skills, and most states require students to pass state competency exams prior to getting a university degree conferred. The conferral of the degree ensures that graduates of state approved teacher prep programs addresses the skills teachers need to be certified. Other countries require similar approaches to initial teacher preparation programs (Petersen and Treagust 2014).

EDUCATIONAL LEADERSHIP PREPARATORY PROGRAMS

Introduction

The Every Student Succeeds Act (ESSA) (2015) specifically mentions the importance of school and district leaders in reaching student outcome goals, and allows states and districts to use federal funds to support activities that are innovative and lead initiatives that improve the skills and knowledge of school leaders (Herman et al. 2016).

The Wallace Foundation has long been a supporter of school leader development programs. This national philanthropy gives grants to university and district partners to develop principal pipeline programs. The Wallace Foundation Report entitled "Improving University Principal Preparation Programs" (2016) described five focused themes of consideration. One of those five themes is a focus on critical university-district partnerships that embed the need of practitioners into high-quality preparatory programs at universities.

The Professional Standards for Education Leaders (2015), formerly known as Interstate School Leadership Licensure Consortium (ISLLC), (Council of Chief State School Officers) are the basis for growth of educational leader preparatory programs, and should drive the program components of university programs. The members of the National Policy Board for Educational Administration is comprised of practitioners at the K–12 level and university level through numerous national organizations. These organizations include the American Association of School Administrators (AASA); the American Association of Colleges of Teacher Education (AACTE); the Council of Chief School Officers (CCSSO); the Council for the Accreditation of Educator Preparation (CAEP); the National School Boards Association (NSBA); and the University Council for Educational Administration (UCEA) to name a few.

COLLABORATION

The Council for the Accreditation of Educator Preparation (CAEP) is an organization that is creating a national forum to raise standards for educator preparation programs based on impact on student success. At the national conference held in Washington, D.C., in September 2016, a focus on partnership development was announced as a significant area of research for the organization.

The purpose of these standards is to have a framework for partnership work between universities, research and practitioners, and to create policy that guides programs of study and supports principal pipeline programs in schools and districts.

PRACTICAL IMPLICATIONS OF PARTNERSHIPS

Examples shared thus far indicate many types of university and community partnerships and how they were created, who they serve, and why they matter. How do these partnerships foster successive leadership, leadership capacity, and sustainability of effective leadership through collaboration?

Helping individuals grow into leaders extends influence of individuals and program impact (Maxwell 2013). The best chance for sustaining organization success is by building leadership capacity within the organization. The decision to support and establish these practices enables a cycle of continuous feedback and growth.

Evaluation of capacity through Communities of Learning, Inquiry and Practice (CLIPs) as defined by Parsons et al. (Fall 2016) is applicable to university partnerships. This form of a community of practice through a model of professional learning communities was the result of a national reform movement of educators, policy makers, colleges, and community partners with the intent of helping community college students succeed.

These authors described the application of the CLIPs model at a community college and a medical school, one in the United States and one in Canada. They reported that both institutions utilized the structure to generate inquiry-based practice and was successful in both settings. Positive cultural and organizational change resulted, and a critical component was a systemic approach to connecting the goals of the organization with shared interests.

Hopson, Miller, and Lovelace (2016) reported that university-school-community partnerships are strong supporters of constituencies that can work together to support change in communities. The information shared regarding police training and assistance with communities could help drive program components in criminal justice and business programs and graduate leaders who can blend needs across disciplines in leadership roles.

Human services by nature identify aspects of non-profit agencies and how partnerships benefit students, community residents and groups, and individuals in communities. The integration of support and training from university programs, graduates, and organizations incorporates characteristics of partnership success.

Criminal justice programs and policing support partnership growth and leadership development. When communities are at odds with police authorities, leaders in the community emerge to assist in finding shared resolutions to identified problems. Students in university programs need to develop these leadership skills, as do practitioners in the field.

In all branches of the military, leadership is focused upon and developed at all stages, including at the cadet level, training, evaluation, and implementation during deployment missions. The National Defense Authorization Act required the Department of Defense to build a performance-based evaluation system that supports leadership development (Taylor 2015). Air force, navy, coast guard, army, and marines have all identified the importance of developing and sustaining leaders through research, support, critical analysis, problem solving, and decision making strategies that are the same as those in the business, education, criminal justice, and human services arenas (Storlie 2015). The transference of these leadership skills to civilian positions enable many veterans to be successful through university programs of study.

In the corporate world, partnerships and collaboration are often minimized by some due to the competitive nature of a capitalistic society. However, organizations like Google, Apple, and Facebook demonstrated how teamwork benefits organizations. Good decision making allows organizational leaders to meet and exceed goals (Beshears and Gino 2014). Studies in the areas of manufacturing, banking, consulting, health care, among others, employ basic principles of economics, as psychologists describe. Human characteristics are the core of organizational decisions.

In the *Harvard Business Review* (May 2015) there is a collection of articles of how collaborative work support organizational growth and goals. It is interesting to note that in these articles, a plan for a cycle of systemic growth and evaluation is exactly the same as educational and school improvement plans. Identifying a problem, the root of the problem, engaging people in the organization to identify steps to remediate, a system of evaluation, and a cycle of continuous feedback based on results applies to all organizations and schools.

KEY IDEAS IN THIS CHAPTER

- Integrated community partnerships can be in all university disciplines

- Service projects transcend departments and programs and can successfully engage all stakeholders
- Students can become leaders through various partnerships
- Community agencies and organizations benefit for partnerships
- Critical analysis and higher level thinking skills are embedded in partnership activities
- Engagement of stakeholders creates organizational trust

SUMMARY

The recognition of similarities across disciplines in university programs supports a commonality of support for establishing programs in many schools in higher education that develop leaders. Every organization needs to build capacity of effective leaders in order for their programs to grow. Students in all disciplines need to develop skills of teamwork, problem solving, using data to inform and meet institutional goals, and build and sustain relationships to support and facilitate missions of the organization.

Chapter Three

K–12 School Partnerships

Fern Aefsky, Jodi Lamb, David Laroche, Renee Sedlack, and Toni Zetsche

The Blueprint for Reform (March 2010) was a proposal for change for the federal government's reauthorization of the Elementary and Secondary Act. This document reflected a change setting high standards and measuring success or lack thereof based on student achievement as measured on standardized tests developed by each state to a national focus on curriculum standards, and "a framework to guide our deliberations and shared work—with parents, students, educators, business and community leaders, elected officials, and other partners—to strengthen America's public education system" (Obama 2010).

The importance of supporting and celebrating innovative approaches to teaching and learning and to evaluate what works well in America's schools was a vital component of this reform movement. The goal for the nation's schools is to reward success rather than identifying failures and to recognize progress and growth rather than using a single factor (assessment results).

As stated in chapter 1, the new Every Student Succeeds Act (ESSA) is the U.S. Department of Education's law that recognizes the gap between policy makers and practitioners. ESSA contains specific language requiring partnerships between K–12 schools, universities, parents, and community organizations, as a way to support student achievement and success for all. The areas of focus for university partnerships and K–12 schools include: policy; research; professional development, mentoring (adults and students), instructional leadership (teacher and administrative); and family involvement.

Input from all stakeholders and integration of resources will allow us to better understand the needs of practitioners and further develop partnerships while facilitating a discussion surrounding the benefits of collaborative partnerships with school districts and K–12 educators. The importance of representatives from diverse organizations to collaborate requires a process of communicating and agreeing on shared goals, methods of implementing various projects, and establishing roles and responsibilities of stakeholders from each organization (Wasonga, Rari, and Wanzare 2011). Interest in initiating, maintaining, and sustaining these partnerships requires leadership skill in the organizations involved.

POLICY

Legislative actions involving educational issues are a state function guided by federal laws. Flexibility exists in some areas and thus various states create legislation that creates policies and regulations in education, both at the K–12 and postsecondary levels. School leaders deal with administrative policies, governance with board members, education market structures, and leadership capacity and development (Tienken and Mullen 2016). How policy decisions impact leadership roles, responsibilities, and development should be considerations of successful partnerships and collaborative efforts between universities and school districts. Variance by state, by policy, and by practice greatly influences opportunities for successful collaboration and can cause changes in program development and implementation.

Special education laws and regulations support school/university/family partnerships. Family-school-community collaborative partnerships are supported by The Individuals with Disabilities Education Act (2004) legislation which mandates the involvement of parents in all decision making of children with disabilities. The Individual with Disability Education Act ensures services for students with disabilities from birth to twenty-one years of age. This law entitles students with disabilities to a free, appropriate public education.

Students with certain disabilities in postsecondary education, such as attention deficit hyperactivity disorder, may be eligible for services under Section 504 of the Rehabilitation Act. This law provides a different level of services and support for students and will be discussed in detail in chapter 5.

RESEARCH

The Professional Standards for Educational Leaders (2015) guide educational policies as they describe a national agreement of the outcomes educational leaders in university programs of study should exhibit upon completions of such programs. These standards are research-based and support the relationship between student achievement and leadership of schools.

Schools (public, private, and parochial) provide the perfect setting for putting theory into practice for university professors. University level researchers can create powerful partnerships that engage current practitioners and improve the quality of beginning teacher leaders and administrative leaders at the school and district levels. This type of collaborative partnership may increase retention through professional development training, mentoring, and gaining resources (i.e., grants) while allowing the school setting to provide the setting for shared research.

Research supports the importance of building relationships within the school community and between community entities (Simons and Friedman 2008; REL 2009; Sepaniou 2009). Clark (2007) identified the competing purposes or functions of schools and how values affect curriculum, learning activities, and both the internal and external culture of schools. He stated that the public needs to understand the challenge that school administrators face as they attempt to engage children in the learning process while designating staff to support student needs and allocating resources appropriately.

Research has been the traditional connection between universities and school districts. However, traditionally, researchers use the school setting as a laboratory. The characteristics of collaborative analysis, decision making, work, and distribution of results was a university researcher function, not the function of school leaders.

When research is done as a partnership activity, stakeholders from both organizations work together to formulate an action research plan. Data analysis, data informed decision making, implementation, resources, evaluation and dissemination of information are shared between organizations. Leaders from both organizations must support the work and the resulting information as part of an ongoing cycle of feedback and improvement. This is one way leaders can maximize and manage human capital (Odden 2011).

When practitioners are involved as partners in research, leadership capacity is developed. Shared presentations, articles, and work become a leadership skill that teachers and administrators can accomplish. Without the assistance and guidance from university partners, this type of leadership activity would be less likely to occur.

Most people view research as an activity reserved for scientists who take precise steps in gathering data and applying statistical analysis to interpret that data for the rest of the world. In the discussion of increasing parent involvement in schools, we learn that research can be a simple and unifying effort of parents and school leaders. When viewed from the participatory action research perspective (Freire 1995), we recognize immediately that research can and should be a major activity of parent-school groups. Participatory Action Research (PAR) becomes the process through which parents and school leaders begin to raise questions together and learn from their collaborative efforts to answer those questions. This is also known as cooperative inquiry.

The conceptual base of cooperative inquiry or PAR is to research "with" rather than "on" people. Cooperative inquiry emphasizes that all active participants are fully involved in research decisions as co-researchers. It also changes the school-parent dynamic to one that is balanced, equal, and operating on a level plane. Parents and school leaders share the role of researcher and participant together. The knowledge that comes with shared action research serves to unify parents and school officials in ways that could not have previously existed.

It is through the process of sharing information and experiences with a group that the members learn from each other, and have an opportunity to develop a shared understanding of their mutual goals. Wanat (2010) suggests that schools might consider having parents engage in action research projects with children and keep journals with teachers as a means of increasing parent involvement.

There are numerous examples of the process of PAR in school community settings. Let's examine one case that serves to illustrate the power of PAR and the key elements of leading partnerships and effecting change. The case example took place in a small city school district serving a large, mostly poor population of students and families. A Shared Decision Making Committee, comprised of school officials and select parents, took on the task of increasing parent involvement in school activities. The question before the committee was "what can be done to improve parent participation in their child's education?" The goal seemed simple enough but the road to asking and answering that question created numerous and challenging ideas, conjectures, discussions, and thoughts about the issue of parent involvement.

Questions emerged such as: What does parent involvement mean? How much parent involvement is appropriate? Does parent involvement change as children progress through elementary, middle, and high school? What are the most important issues that parents have about their child's education? What are the barriers to parent involvement? What are teachers' perspectives on parent involvement? How do school administrators manage parent involvement? In action research, questions like this are clear indicators that true inquiry is emerging.

PROFESSIONAL DEVELOPMENT

Data and questions about data take place concurrently with each bit of new knowledge building upon the previous information and moving the questions from general initial analysis to more focused inquiry and analysis. The action that is generated is the goal for the school leader.

Collaborative partnerships and characteristics for success were identified by Baker and Pifer (2011). Boston Public Schools created a historical partnership professional development series. Through creative scheduling and working with local museums, the district's social studies department developed a list of opportunities for PD sessions that were held either after school or on Saturday. The exciting part is that several museums extended services to students so that if a teacher attended the training, s/he received a free field trip for their students. Not only did the teachers learn how to add primary sources into their instruction, but their enthusiasm for the topic grew (Dunne 2016).

According to Dunne, "The series exemplifies a best practice in the field: it is a program that can be offered at little to no cost and can be easily replicated in other cities and towns that have multiple historic sites and community partner resources. We believe that the outcomes of the program—deeper teacher knowledge of the diverse heritage and history of Boston's many communities, strengthened bonds between BPS and local historic and cultural organizations, and modeling the use of 'place-based education' with teachers in a way that they can re-create with their students—yield great fruit as both a rich adult learning experience and as a hands-on pedagogical training" (Dunne 2016, n.p).

Examples of partnership strategies that were generated by looking for ways to create established best practices in education while developing successful practices that include place-based education, transitional partnerships, and mentoring. The first strategy creates a unique spin on place-based education. "Place-based education immerses students in local heritage, culture, ecology, landscapes, opportunities, and experiences as a foundation for the study of language arts, mathematics, social studies, science, and other subjects. Place-based education encourages teachers and students to use the schoolyard, community, public lands, and other special places as resources, turning communities into classrooms" (Place-based Education Evaluation Collaborative 2010, p. 2).

The Place-based Education Evaluation Collaborative has conducted research over the last several years to determine the effectiveness of this educational approach. According to the researchers, "the findings are clear: place-based education fosters students' connection to place and creates vibrant partnerships between schools and communities. It boosts student achievement and improves environmental, social, and economic vitality" (Place-based Education Evaluation Collaborative 2010, p. 2).

This strategy explores how place-based education can serve as a powerful model for professional development while building school partnerships. What would happen if a school planned professional development around access to a local museum? How would it impact curriculum design and the instructional strategies used in the classrooms?

Gardner (2011) reported on the successful STEM (science, technology, engineering, and mathematics) research completed at Illinois State University and the effectiveness of the partnership projects with university's and K–12 schools. Students in the K–12 schools are exposed to and participate in STEM projects and teachers are able to benefit from professional development training from faculty with expertise in STEM areas of study.

The nation faces a probable shortage of school leaders when the current group of baby boomers continues to retire creating a staggering 40 percent turnover in the coming years (Spiro, Mattis, and Mitgang 2007). With years of experience and a deep understanding of the role, our nation is losing a collective set of skills and expertise.

Spiro, et al. concluded "the harsh truth is that the new school leader faces a dizzying array of tasks associated with managing a highly complex organization: from budgeting and busing to discipline, personnel and union matters and public relations" (2017). The report emphasizes, "Professional development of new principals is a worthwhile public investment."

Professional development of higher education faculty is one benefit of collaborative professional development (Ness et al. 2010). They reported, after a three-year study, that a collaborative approach to professional development benefits those faculty members teaching in institutes of higher education (IHE) and impacts teaching and other collaborative efforts through partnerships, both at and between university programs and with other partners.

Penn State had a professional development partnership with an area school district, and was awarded the first National Association for Professional Development School Achievement Award in 2009 (Nolan et al. 2009). This was an acknowledgment of the importance of IHE and school partnerships in professional development training. The faculty and staff of the school district gained skills and knowledge through this partnership.

MENTORING

Mentoring has become a term used for establishing partnerships between professionals in both K–12 and university settings. At both levels, mentors are assigned to new faculty members so that there is a partnership beyond supervisors.

In order to develop the next generation of leaders, universities and school districts need to recognize the long-term benefits of mentoring. It is evident that school districts need to invest in the future leaders of our schools in order to foster strong student achievement, address the needs of a diverse student population, and insure that business and community partnerships are developed and nurtured. There are many hopeful signs that there is a growing interest in seriously investing in school leadership.

Faculty members at universities are assigned someone who can assist in processes, policies, and teaching. At the K–12 level, teachers are assigned teacher mentors and administrators are assigned mentors who have the same job function (assistant principal, principal, director, or supervisor). In all cases, the purpose of the mentoring is to establish both an organizational and job connection with support for success.

K–12 MENTORING

There has been a significant shift in the roles and responsibilities of the school principal. The job has become more demanding and complex, requiring longer hours and diversified skills in order to meet additional challenges and requirements of both a changing society and governmental focus on academic accountability.

The postmodern principal needs to develop the capacity to put learning first, implement change when needed, and have the courage to make decisions in the best interest of students (Spiro, Mattis, and Mitgang 2007). While the absence of data to determine the effects of mentoring make it difficult to discuss its value, it is widely understood by school leaders that "no matter what preparation anyone has, being the principal is not the same. Nothing prepares you for the job" (Spiro, Mattis, and Mitgang 2007).

Jim Hull (2012), Center for Public Education's senior policy analyst, asserted, "Principals are now more than ever focused on student achievement while still retaining their traditional administrative and building manager duties. Because of this, principals typically work 10 hour days and many believe the job is just not 'doable' as it is configured now."

The postmodern principal's essential performance roles have evolved to reflect changes in the American family. Recognizing the relationship of family involvement to student achievement, research suggests that principals set the tone for the school, provide an atmosphere for collaboration between partners, and help both teachers and parents gain the skills to work together effectively for student success (Parent Involvement Center 2012).

Principals need to know how to work with a variety of populations, use the skills of public relations professionals, and understand the importance of building strong family relationships. In addition, aspiring leaders are younger in age than their retiring baby boomer counterparts when first undertaking the challenging task of becoming a school principal. Joanne Rooney, co-director of the Midwest Principal's Center noted that the challenges that educators face include a focus on accountability for student achievement, special education policies, providing for diverse student populations, and dealing with parents who have had difficulty with systems of bureaucracy (Rooney 2008).

The changing face of the American family, and the very definition of family, often involves risk factors related to life events that result in children residing in environments not conducive to mental well-being or social stability. The majority of American children live in two-parent households; however, according to census reports, that percentage has been steadily decreasing since the 1960s. About 69 percent of children live with two parents (biological or stepparents), 22 percent live with only their mother, 4 percent live with only their father, and 4 percent live with neither parent (U.S. Department of Health and Human Services 2000).

According to the American Psychological Association (2014), "The nation's economic crisis has deeply affected the lives of millions of Americans. Skyrocketing foreclosures and job layoffs have pulled the rug out from under many families, particularly those living in low-income communities. Deepening poverty is inextricably linked with rising levels of homelessness and food insecurity/hunger for many Americans and children are particularly affected by these conditions."

How do new principals acquire the skills and knowledge to address the complexities of their position? April Peters (2010), in her article "Elements of Successful Mentoring of a Female School Leader," noted, "With the amount of new and talented principals that is needed immediately, administrative preparation programs, which contribute significantly to the administrator pipeline, should attempt to address, support, and prepare diverse pools of talented leaders to meet the challenges facing today's schools" (Peterson 2002).

She contends that newly appointed principals are inadequately prepared to meet the demands of their leadership roles. The need to understand how to apply learned theory into practice, how to juggle an array of situations requiring attention, and how to cope with the needs and personalities of children and adults may be a daunting task for the beginner. The focus on rapid decision making, often involving complex issues, has contributed to the stress facing young leaders.

Research supports the value of mentors for beginning principals. John Holloway (2004) emphasized the necessity of an effective principal mentoring program to combat the feelings of isolation and frustration. While many school districts have formal mentoring programs for beginning teachers, there is a lack of similar support for new principals. Often, principals will receive assistance once they are failing; the need for a more proactive approach is critical.

Hall (2008) discussed the need for on-the-job mentoring for new leaders as they begin to apply theory into practice:

> The continuation of this learning process as the teacher then ventures into school administration, however, has been erratic and inconsistent. Now, in the 21st century, in the midst of the Era of Accountability, the need to develop

principals as master artisans is as dire as it is immediate. Unfortunately, we
have often asked aspiring and new principals to go it alone.

The research findings of Lashway (2003) support the notion that the stress
caused by the technical demands of the position along with meeting the
demands of a variety of stakeholders leave principals feeling inadequate
(Holloway 2004). In a survey of ninety-eight principals, researchers learned
that many beginning principals learn their jobs through on-the-job training.
They cited the necessity for the opportunity for sharing their experiences
with experienced colleagues to reduce their feelings of isolation (Holloway
2004). A second study conducted by the Educational Research Service con-
firmed this need for collegial support. One obstacle to this strategy is the time
limits for both the mentor and mentee to spend quality time in reflection and
discussion.

The Wallace Foundation collected research from their projects of principal pipeline development and reported five key themes learned from the field
(Wallace 2016). One of the themes entitled "The course of study at preparation programs does not always reflect principals' real jobs" (Walbiu 2016, p.
9) compiled information from the American Association of School Administrators and superintendents. Data revealed that courses of leadership in IHE
should be taught by instructors with practitioner experience, with a focus on
real-life situations via case studies, field experiences, and role play opportunities.

CHARACTERISTIC OF SUCCESSFUL
MENTORING PARTNERSHIPS

With the compelling need to support new principals in the field, researchers
have examined existing programs to define best practices in the mentoring
partnership. The notion of mentoring is to support new principals in their
own setting as they learn their jobs, rather than watching someone else do it
(Peters 2010). One key component is the need for mentors to spend quality
time with the mentee (Holloway 2004). School districts may choose from
several models of implementation: offering release time for the principal
mentor; or utilizing the expertise of recently retired principals who have
proven records of success as examples.

There needs to be a commitment to identify and train potential mentors.
Spiro, Mattis, and Mitgang (2004) emphasized, "The mere fact that a person
has been a successful principal is no guarantee that he or she will be a
successful mentor." The idea of moving principals from dependence to independence requires a mentor with an array of interpersonal skills. Mentors
need to be focused listeners, have the ability to provide targeted feedback

designed to be non-judgmental, and offer thoughts to enable to mentee to self-reflect.

STUDENT MENTORING

Many schools have a mentoring program. The specific components of each program can vary widely, but in the end it is a "win" if a strong relationship has been established that promotes student achievement. Australia has a mentoring program geared to help indigenous students make the successful transition to college. The AIME program is based upon three legs: storytelling, challenging environment, and aligning positive associations with identity (Priestly et al. 2015). This program has grown in numbers due to its huge success. Students are more likely to graduate (1.87 times more) by participating in the AIME program (Priestly et al. 2015). Schools can use a similar approach to develop their own mentoring program. One elementary school in the central part of Florida connected with the local Kiwanis club to find mentors. The mentors committed to one visit per week and helped the student with math or reading while developing a relationship with the student.

Another school tapped the services of a local retirement village. Some of the residents mentored and others volunteered in the classrooms or media center. Those who were not able to physically go to the school helped with fund raising and finding donations for school supplies and uniforms. The children produced thank you notes and residents were invited for school events and performances.

The administration attended several community meetings at the village to answer questions about the impact of legislation and accountability so that the residents felt better informed and could confidently make their voices heard in the political arena. It was a "win" for both the school and the retirement village.

Another option for a mentoring program is to connect with local companies who have the content expertise in an area that schools intend to develop. For example, if a school is planning to become a STEM academy, then look for mentors in places where there are many engineers. The power or energy company is a great example. The company employs many scientists and engineers so the background knowledge for math and science is significant on the part of the mentors.

If a school has moved from STEM to STEAM, consider local music stores and art supply places. At one school, the partnership began just by asking some of the engineers and scientists to help score the science fair projects and to help out with a few items in the science lab. After using that opportunity to talk about the struggles the students had, the enthusiasm they had for science, and the plan the school had for implementing a STEM program, the power company employees were open to the idea of mentoring some of the neediest students. The goals of the mentoring were quite similar to the Australia model.

TEACHER MENTORS

Many schools assign new teachers to experienced teachers in the same discipline as mentors for the first few years of a new teacher's career. Mentors assist teachers in learning "the ropes" of the school and district, and also serve as a coach for instruction, data collection, and data analysis.

Mentors are typically volunteers who want to help new teachers be successful. However, training for mentors is often limited or non-existent. There is an opportunity for teacher leaders to be developed as mentors, and the ability of universities to help train the mentors as part of teacher and educational leadership prep programs.

In addition, mentors should participate in training to enhance their relationship building and collaborative skills (Holloway 2004). Holloway also notes that it is important as well to match mentor and mentee for compatibility with an understanding of confidentiality and trust. Peters (2010) stressed the importance of a strong relationship so that the mentor can provide welcome guidance and feedback. Finally, mentors should model the problem solving process for their mentees, rather than solving problems for them (Peters 2010).

IMPLICATIONS

An effective mentoring program can greatly ameliorate the isolation felt by new administrators. (Holloway 2004)

The Wallace Foundation suggests that mentors have high quality training. Their report contends that investing in developing new principals is a fiscal priority since the cost of turning around failing schools is greater both financially and academically (Spiro, Mattis, and Mitgang 2007).

A successful program enables mentors to guide mentees not only to understand the complexity of the job but also to understand their ability to lead (Peters 2010). While many states have implemented programs to address the need to mentor new principals, many or most are falling short of their potential (Spiro, Mattis, and Mitgang 2007).

UNIVERSITY COLLABORATION

Many of the attributes identified above are the same for administrators and teachers in K–12 schools as in (IHE). Successful mentoring programs require a commitment of resources to support mentors and mentees, and an identification of the need for new members of the university community to be mentored.

The Wallace Foundation has awarded multiple grants that support partnerships between school districts and universities to build a capacity of school leaders. Successful partnerships between universities and school districts to build and develop programs for developing school administrators are their priority. Local and national professional learning communities are an important component of the grants awarded and practice.

The Association for Colleges for Teacher Education (ACTE) and the American Association of School Administrators (AASA), the School Superintendents Association, and the University Council for Educational Administrators (UCEA) investigated the state of university education principal preparation programs. The Wallace Foundation reviewed the findings from each report, and identified five themes of priorities, one of which was that strong district-university partnerships were essential to produce leaders of K–12 schools (Wallace Foundation, Mendels ed. 2016).

The ACTE report identified the need for high quality mentors for principals. Mentoring by both IHE faculty members and K–12 clinical practice internship supervisors was necessary. Clinical experience is important for school-based administrators and IHE programs that work together with school districts to identify and prepare practitioners better than candidates who do not get similar experiences in their IHE program.

The AASA report indicated that superintendents surveyed endorsed a connection between faculty at IHE and the ability of those faculty to have K–12 experience in order to teach in an educational leadership program of study (CCSS 2012). Some states require this (New York, Florida, California, and Maryland) and practitioners strongly emphasized the need for this important connection between practice and preparation programs.

INSTRUCTIONAL LEADERSHIP

Introduction

The Every Student Success Act (ESSA) contains a significant recognition of instructional leaders and maintaining teacher leaders in schools. The differentiation is that teacher leaders remain at the school level as instructional coaches, teacher leaders/mentors, rather than a desire to be administrators. Recognition of this important leadership role in schools is being identified in states, as there are currently twenty-two states that have certification in the area of teacher leadership. Three years ago, only six states had this as a certification area.

Effective leaders recognize that they cannot accomplish great things alone. They acknowledge that leadership capacity is "broadly distributed in the population and is accessible to anyone who has passion and purpose to change things as they are" (Kouzes and Posner 2010, p. 5). All instructional improvement efforts are implemented and monitored through the work done by teacher leaders facilitating Professional Learning Communities (PLC's) workgroups. PLC's have been defined in educational realms as ways for professionals to analyze, discuss, and improve situations (DuFour and Dufour 2013). The creation and resource allocation for this type of collaborative effort builds the capacity of teacher leaders.

IHE seem to be acknowledging the work previously done in K–12 schools and bringing it into the university setting. Researchers seem to be recognizing the implications of collaboration and partnerships from K–12 settings into the university setting through teacher and administrator preparatory programs of study and improving practices of teaching and learning for university students through collaboration (Bryant-Shankin and Brumage 2011; Johnston, Kaufman, and Thompson 2016; Nolan et al., 2009; Rosenberg et al. 2009).

Teachers are a key aspect of building leaders through partnerships. Teacher leadership is important to consider as we plan the redesign of our schools and create effective schools that focus on the priorities of high quality instruction. By providing training to school leaders to deepen knowledge of the district vision of instructional excellence and expertise in observing this vision in each classroom, including alignment of instruction with the standards as well as the instructional framework and shifts or core actions. To do this there has to be an insistence that managerial tasks are secondary to instructional leadership responsibilities. This requires a leadership model that is part of a culture within a school.

Teacher preparatory programs in IHE need to encourage and expect teacher-family-community engagement, involvement and communication (Zeichner et al. 2016). Programs that prepare teachers need to incorporate expectations, experiences, and evaluation of family engagement theories and practice. If IHE embeds these concepts and practices into programs of study, teacher candidates will graduate with skills and expectations of how to engage families and the community in order to help students demonstrate learning outcomes.

Continually leveraging leadership in the building by prioritizing actions and activities that focus on overcoming obstacles to make a difference in student learning. Over time a culture of collaboration focused on learning is achieved. Collaboration can take many forms, from the focus on the individual student to the development of multidisciplinary lessons to the analysis of recent achievement data. Every collaboration meeting must have defined results with specific and measurable adult actions according to Reeves (2009).

In a study of school leadership capacity for lasting school improvement, Linda Lambert, a professor emeritus at California State University, collected data from fifteen schools at all levels that were no longer low-performing schools. After experiencing instructive, transitional, and high leadership capacity phases of growth, teachers journeyed from dependency to high levels of self-organization and demonstrated a readiness to lead a school without a principal (Lambert 2006). Lambert describes leadership capacity as broad-based, skillful participation in the work of leadership (2003). In her description of the constructivist teacher leader, leadership is understood as reciprocal, purposeful learning in community settings.

Exemplary school leaders have a positive impact on increasing teacher collaboration, satisfaction, and leadership (Orphanos and Orr 2014). They found that strong leadership preparation programs supported positive leadership practices that influenced teacher leadership and organizational change. Identified characteristics included the importance of engaging in collaborations or partnerships with various community and school organizations.

The institution of a common language for teachers to use as a framework to work collaboratively is a priority in schools. Collaboration as a form of school leadership used as a tool to improve schools and increase student performance has been identified in numerous studies (Hulpia, Devos, and Van Kerr 2011; Orphanos and Orr 2011; Wallace Foundation 2006).

Instructional leadership identifies leaders that take an active role in the curriculum, the teaching and learning process, and cycle of continual improvement of student outcomes. Boylan (2016) identified the importance of education collaborations and leadership at all levels. He described a "systems leader," defined as someone in a senior leadership position whose leadership skills are distributive and extend beyond the walls of his/her own building.

There has been renewed interest, research, and policy related to instructional leadership. Since 2012, many states have begun a process of determining certification for teacher leaders. The National Teacher Leadership Model Standards were developed in 2014, recognizing the importance of keeping teacher leaders in schools as instructional coaches, professional learning community facilitators, technology and media support, and focused on professional educators who are leaders but do not want to be traditional administrators. This renewed area of focus has resulted in twenty-two states (compared to two years ago) that now have teacher leadership as a separate certification area.

The term instructional leadership often means that the school leader takes on the role of coach working alongside the staff to impact achievement.

Leading teachers and staff in the unpacking of standards, mapping of curriculum, development of unit plans, lesson plans, and assessments aligned with the standards is instructional leadership in a pure form (Chrispeels et al. 2008).

Practitioners often identify themselves as instructional leaders based on characteristics derived from an amalgamation of historical, popular, and emerging literature that seeks to define the role through definitive actions or behaviors. Curriculum and instruction are undoubtedly at the foundation of education and high quality learning and many practitioners are focused on increasing achievement, however, the responsibilities of the twenty-first century leader are far more encompassing.

The shift in thinking that has occurred in relationship to curriculum and instruction allows educators to focus more time and energy on quality instruction that is related to real-world preparation with an emphasis on equity. In 2009, the U.S. Department of Education secretary, Arne Duncan, released regulations known as "Race to the Top" (Ravitch 2010). Common Core has challenged educators to re-evaluate state standards and re-evaluate common practices that were often coined "best practice." This shift or recalibration, has strained both teachers and leaders, as many were not fully prepared to deeply engage in such transparent reflection.

As the worldview on standards-based education shifts into something very different than what it was a decade ago; school leaders are finding that instructional leadership is a blended model of practices and tasks, much less product and much more metacognitive, a reflective practice. As society becomes more global and complex, the needs of educators are becoming increasingly unique. Instructional leadership in the twenty-first century requires a more sophisticated, facilitative approach that focuses on creating a school culture of leaders.

Seeking opportunities for growth beyond the school leader is essential. Instructional leadership at this level requires facilitation of collaborative planning and building capacity in teacher leaders that are knowledgeable in the curriculum and able to effectively lead others.

The school leader can engage in learning and development alongside teachers so that their ability to observe, evaluate, and develop teachers through feedback related to techniques and methods is far more realistic. Blasé and Blasé (2000) suggest instructional leadership in a more facilitative manner that provides support for development opportunities, soliciting opinions, providing feedback and praise and modeling behaviors in place of curriculum knowledge attainment.

In a convergence of leadership theories, the twenty-first century leader must become well versed in understanding how to respond, how to engage teachers in the problem solving process, and how to evaluate instructional practices on a deeper level than simply checking boxes on a required form.

Instructional knowledge is an essential component; however, it is not enough to know the content, it is required to have a comprehensive understanding of the needs of the staff to know and teach content, with accountability and continuous improvement considered throughout delivery of instruction.

With the implementation of the Race to the Top regulations in 2009, the initiation of national Common Core Standards and a shift in thinking, practitioners often struggled to develop a comprehensive desire to lead. School leaders today face an insurmountable task to keep up with curriculum and fully understand the standards in a way that truly allows for coaching and development.

Through the use of Professional Learning Communities, school principals can make both teacher and student learning a priority in a collaborative leadership process. Instructional leadership as defined by the National Association of Elementary School Principals (2001) is "leading learning communities." This definition provides an approach to leading through collaborative problem solving.

Taking a more realistic approach to evolving into effective instructional leadership through collaborative practice, a true convergence of styles must occur to create a climate that can survive the shift through the demands of the state and local government as they "transform" various programs and implement new initiatives. Leadership under the current climate of education calls for an integrated approach that blends organizational leadership, instructional leadership, adaptive leadership and management, while utilizing components of kinetic or affilitative leadership.

Both kinetic and affilitative leadership styles are both centered on a foundation of trust and building strong professional relationships. A diverse approach is necessary as the curriculum becomes more rigorous and integrated in real-world learning opportunities that extend beyond the walls of the classroom. Many schools today are over-managed and under-led, meaning that the day-to-day business of education is organized while motivation and cultivation of trust and relationships are secondary

Madden, Lynch, and Doe (2015) referenced studies on educational organizational behavior among successful leaders.

- Effective instructional leaders need to be resource providers. It is not enough for principals to know the strengths and weaknesses of their faculties; they must also recognize teachers' desires to be acknowledged and appreciated for a job well done.
- Effective instructional leaders need to be instructional resources. Teachers count on their principals as resources of information on current trends and effective instructional practices. Instructional leaders are tuned in to issues relating to curriculum, effective pedagogical strategies, and assessment.

- Effective instructional leaders need to be good communicators. They need to communicate essential beliefs regarding learning, such as the conviction that all children can learn.
- Effective instructional leaders need to create a visible presence. This includes focusing on learning objectives, modeling behaviors of learning, and designing programs and activities on instruction.

The skills identified and further strengthened by Madden, Lynch, and Doe (2015) provide a foundation for instructional leadership that encourages a strong focus on the human aspect of organizational growth. Emphasis on the productivity or achievement through positive human interaction and facilitation of growth opportunity is at the core of cognitive studies related to human learning and organizational growth.

Organizational behavior according to Owens and Valesky (2007) is defined as "a field of social-scientific study and application to administrative practice that seeks to understand and use knowledge of human behavior in social and cultural setting for the improvement of organizational performances" (p. 259). The study of leadership within an organization often uncovers a plethora of styles that attempt to define characteristics of leadership.

The characteristics of a good leader are a fusion of purposeful behaviors that blend well with the personalities, needs, and behaviors of those they lead. Of course certain behaviors and characteristics yield desirable outcomes and should be recognized as valuable, however, can we really assume that any one style of leadership or management is most effective in every circumstance? Can we assume that bureaucratic leadership has no place in education? Determining which style will illicit the most desirable student outcomes is a matter of knowing the organization, the staff, and the student population.

Educational researchers such as Hallinger and Heck (1996), Owens and Valesky (2007), Waters, Marzano, and McNulty (2004) share a common theme related to the impact of the instructional leader on student achievement in that each identifies that a correlation exists, yet the impact is often difficult to measure due to variables that are often uncontrollable by the leader. According to Marzano and Waters (2013) high performing schools typically had strong instructional leadership, which included a climate focused on a common goal, a system of clear standards and clear expectations for student learning through instructional shifts, and strong leadership willing to monitor the level of rigor that occurs in the classroom.

In a metaanalysis conducted by Robinson, Lloyd, and Rowe (2008), research looked at twenty-two of the twenty-seven studies involved in the comparison of transformational and instructional leadership on student achievement. Research derived from the metaanalysis suggested that on average, the impact of instructional leadership on student achievement was three to four times greater than that of transformational leadership.

The impact of school leadership on student achievement will consistently yield a variety of results as schools are unique living, breathing, and ever changing organizations with variables that are difficult to replicate. This is often difficult to measure through the impact on culture can often produce indicators that weigh on achievement and teacher retention based on support in the classroom (Mitchell, Kensler, and Tschannen-Moran 2015).

Many school leaders are taxed with the daily operations leaving the instructional leadership to teacher leaders who cultivate relationships with staff, collaborate and build the culture either positively or negatively depending on their leadership abilities. Leadership in today's society requires strong awareness and ability in all of the components of an integrated leadership framework to support both students and staff.

As a twenty-first century leader, it is important to be able to tackle difficult issues with confidence and quick decision making when necessary, while also being able to recognize when to step back and allow the team to tackle the issues through collaborative problem-solving. Managing is necessary, leading is essential. Providing school staff with the ability to identify, analyze, and overcome is derived from creating a positive culture, providing the staff with professional development that creates a strong awareness, then trusting that they are capable of decision-making that supports the vision and mission of the school.

The organizational climate of the organization should be one that is based on shared goals and values between managers and employees (Barsh and Lavoie 2014). For a school community to work well, it must achieve agreement in each role relationship in terms of the understandings held about these personal obligations and expectations of others. Relational trust in building effective educational communities refers to an interrelated set of mutual dependencies embedded within the social exchanges of any school community. Regardless of how much formal power any given role has in a school community (student to teacher, teacher to teacher, or teacher to principal), all participants remain dependent on others to achieve desired outcomes and feel empowered by their efforts (Bryk 2003).

Compensation, certification, and recognition and retention of great teachers and leaders is a focus of a national agenda. AASA, CAEP, ISLLC, and other professional organizations have brought these discussions to their conferences, asking presenters and participants how they do, or want to, reward great teachers and leaders and define challenges in their systems to actualizing a system of support.

The practice of instructional leadership is anything but simple and its characteristics are fluid and evolving as new obstacles arise and educator needs shift. The goal of school leadership hinges on making schools truly inclusive with a focus on student outcomes (McLeskey and Waldron 2015).

A principal of a high school reported that when he began his career in the late 1990s, a partnership between the University of South Florida and his school was in place as the school opened to organize the school around the Learning Community concept. The principal and various other district personnel were interested in the notion that teachers could be more successful and better engage students if the entire school were organized to support the concept of learning communities. Prior to the opening of the school the teachers that were hired were given the opportunity to train on the merits of learning communities where teachers plan curriculum around a career area of interest promoted heavily at the time through the literature.

A priority for this type of schoolwide structure was the need for teachers to be able to collaborate regularly around a vision and using a common language that all teachers understand and are comfortable in groups. At a school that was brand new and where teachers were handpicked for their abilities as great teachers, the background and training was not provided for the endeavor to be successful. Teachers were frustrated with their inability to adapt the concepts of the learning community idea to the everyday classroom whose structure was at this time very traditional. University programs to train teachers were not providing students with the tools that they needed to be teachers in a system that would require them to plan together in groups of common interest for their students.

Principals do make a difference in student learning, and the most powerful strategy for having a positive impact on that learning is to facilitate the learning of the educators who serve those students through the PLC process (DuFour 2011). As stated in the Wallace Foundation Report (2016), partnerships with IHE in the development and implementation of leader preparation programs provides support and leadership opportunities for both the IHE and continued approval processes for programs in all states, and provides support through professional development and research with K–12 school partners that positively impacts student learning.

KEY IDEAS IN THIS CHAPTER

- Policy impact on partnerships within IHE and between IHE and K–12 schools
- Research and partnership benefits to IHE and K–12 school personnel
- Professional development opportunities through collaborative partnerships that strengthen leadership capacity
- Mentoring as support for stakeholders in both IHE and K–12 schools, with business and community partners

- Instructional leadership as concept for creating and sustaining excellent teachers and leaders at both the university and K–12 school setting
- Leadership challenges and support can be shared through effective partnerships

SUMMARY

Szczesiul and Huizenga (2014) described leadership as a struggle to facilitate and support collaboration, future leaders, and as a significant factor in determining if professional collaboration and partnerships occur. There is a mutual benefit to university and K–12 partners, which supports multiple levels of leadership. Shared organizational goals and resources provide opportunities for stakeholders to develop collaborative work that benefits each organization, faculty, and community members, and develops strong leaders through the shared work.

Chapter Four

Family Partnerships and Engagement

Frank Mulhern and Fern Aefsky

Parent and family involvement and engagement are important partnerships that need to be nurtured and supported. Collaborative partnerships in institutions of higher education (IHE) and K–12 schools with families and the community warrant action from leaders. An opportunity to foster and develop leaders through family partnerships is also evident. Parents can be engaged as educational leaders through collaborative projects where they share their knowledge and expertise in order to improve educational attributes of the system (Ishimaru 2014).

Building partnerships between school, home, and community is the responsibility of school leaders. Parental empowerment is a key component for sustainability (Colombo 2004).

Sustainability comes through prolonged and continuous efforts. Epstein (2001) stated that in a caring school community, "participants work continually to improve the nature and effects of partnerships" (p. 406). Without active and leading partnerships, even caring school communities will regress and decline.

According to Epstein (2001), decline of parent involvement occurs almost automatically across grades as students move into middle and high school years. It appears, too, that single parents, and especially fathers, are less involved in school activities. In economically stressed districts there is also a tendency for school contact with parents to center around student problems rather than positive issues. Sustaining partnerships requires insight and knowledge that helps school leaders to develop and guide the process of collaboration.

LEADERSHIP DEVELOPMENT

Through various partnerships, leaders develop skills through practice. Parents are included in this possibility, as the relationships of parents in schools support facilitation of creating leaders. When organization leaders facilitate stakeholder engagement, involvement, and leadership, new leaders emerge from those collaborative efforts.

UNIVERSITIES

If you are a parent of a child going to college since the year 2000, you might have experienced an increased awareness of the importance of a connection between the school, student, and family. Parent weekends, orientation events, communication materials, are offered by colleges and universities at a higher frequency than the previous decades (Lynch 2006).

The importance of involving the family of a student in a higher education facility has demonstrated increased retention and graduation rates (Murphy 2013). She studied parent involvement in college and found a positive relationship between first-year student retention and participation of those students' families in orientation and other school and family events.

Student engagement is supported by family engagement at all ages. While the types of activities may vary, the connections between family, students, and school is evident (Harvard Family Research Project 2010). Students from various background achieve gains in school success when parents are involved (Marshall and Shah 2014).

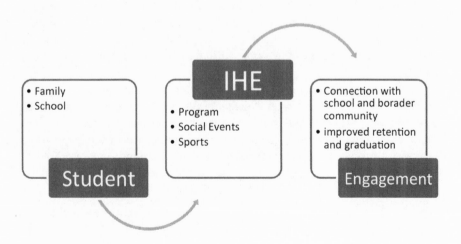

Figure 4.1. Student-Family-School Relationships

Sax and Weintraub (2014) reported the importance of family involvement related to the success of first year college students. The emotional well-being of students and reported success in their first year was identified as directly correlated to the level of interaction with parent and family.

As mentioned in previous chapters, organizations such as: the American Association of School Administrators (AASA); the American Association of Colleges of Teacher Education (AACTE); the Council of Chief School Officers (CCSSO); the Council for the Accreditation of Educator Preparation (CAEP); the National School Boards Association (NSBA); and the University Council for Educational Administration (UCEA) are supportive of and focus attention on bringing K–12 and IHE together in partnership endeavors. These national organizations are trying to bridge the divide that has existed and combine efforts with practitioners to help guide practice, programs, and policy.

Family involvement is one of those endeavors to support student success. Bastian (2010) studied parent involvement at the college level and reported there were increased opportunities for parents to be involved with college processes of recruitment, financial aid, school selection, and problem solving. Financing of schools requires parental involvement and recruiters tend to target marketing toward parents (Lange and Stone 2001).

University faculty and admissions departments can play an active role as one of the community members in parent university/academy programs. As partners, faculty can provide workshops, information about post-high school opportunities, encourage campus visits, and be visible as a helpful organization to the community.

Technology allows for ongoing parental consultation with key issues. Examples include academic planning (faculty, workload), socialization (roommate, events, clubs) that have enhanced the ability for the university and student to communicate frequently to foster parental engagement (Daniel et al. 2001; Forbes 2001; Kepic 2006). The increased opportunities to real time communication keeps parents informed, students supported, and university-family partnerships developed.

K–12 SCHOOLS

School system leaders need to facilitate successful partnerships between parents, school, and community, including IHE, in order to increase student achievement. Improving communication skills between all stakeholders leads to student support systems that allow young people to reach goals and graduate from high school.

Parent-educator partnerships are vital to helping all children succeed (Salopek 2011). Simons and Friedman (2008) cited a lack of parental involvement as a significant issue impacting student achievement and school success. A synthesis of research studies assessing this relationship (Henderson et al. (2007) reviewed fifty-one studies published between 1995 and 2002. They reported that all of the studies found a positive relationship between family and community involvement and increased benefits for students in academic achievement.

These authors also summarized findings that students from all cultural and economic backgrounds demonstrated gains when their parents were involved in their education. This involvement varied by student age/grade; however, the engagement of parents in the educational process demonstrated improved student performance in all grades.

Parental advocacy is something we should want, not oppose. Rudy Crew, then superintendent of Miami-Dade County Public Schools (2008) stated: "parents . . . must learn to be demanding consumers of public education." He believed that schools should welcome parents who challenge district practices on behalf of their children, as this builds a collaborative school culture.

Children are dependent on adults from the time they are born. Trusting adults for safety and security are key aspects as children are nurtured and develop a sense of belonging in their families, community, and schools. Values in leadership support and define the interactions between leaders and their influence on followers (Heifetz 2003). He stated that "leaders not only influence followers but are under their influence as well" (p. 17). This important concept is paramount for school leaders to build improved systems of change which value and encourage partnerships with parents.

A key concept for building and sustaining successful parental partnerships is the ability for leaders to share power (Weiss and Stephen 2009). If families feel welcome in schools, and are truly partners in their child's education success and failures with school personnel, relationships will sustain over time. Parent programs that are not successful often are the result of a lack of a faith that the school building and district leaders truly want to work with parents proactively.

An essential characteristic of successful school leaders is an understanding of how children learn and how to connect the variables impacting the learning process for children. Parental involvement and influence must be encouraged for individual student needs and for the benefit of the school community.

This concept can be applied to the entire school community of leaders: teachers, principals, parents/guardians, and students. The characteristics listed above apply to leadership qualities at every level that support student achievement. Deal and Peterson (1999) defined a school leader who shapes school culture as a visionary. Their definition of a visionary leader was a leader who "works with other leaders and community to define a deeply value-focused picture for the school" (p. 86). Lutz and Merz (1992) described communities as a delicate balance of subcommittees, each with its own set of values, which change on a frequent basis.

Leaders of schools are frequently considered as "good as their last transaction" based on this balance of subcommittees in a community. Many decisions must be made and different constituency groups are happy (or not) at any given point.

For example, if a school district is geographically in a cold climate and winter weather impacts school openings, on a given day parents may be angry that there is a delay, as a child's changing schedule impact their work responsibilities, teachers may be angry that school is open if weather is bad, forgetting that most workers in the community are expected to work, and students are disappointed that they do not have a day off. Now imagine that teachers and students were happy because schools were closed, parents may still be unhappy because of child supervision challenges, and all are angry when the days missed in the winter have to be made up during the intended spring break.

Expanding leadership decisions into curriculum and instructional areas, personnel, professional development, accountability to the board and community, and extracurricular programs and the difficulty of decisions supporting all stakeholders all the time is further diminished. Visionary leaders plan and communicate the value-based decisions that support community priorities and school goals.

Parental support of school programs is an important value to nurture in all communities. Parents are advocates for their children, and need to have opportunities to ask questions, understand priorities, share opinions, and believe they are being listened to by school personnel. Parents loan us their children every day, expecting them to be safe, learn, and be able to demonstrate that knowledge in a positive academic and social environment.

School leaders must acknowledge the relationship between adults on behalf of the children. Building positive ways to communicate children's success is a critical part of fostering school/home relationships. School leaders must also recognize relationships between adults on behalf of their faculty and staff members.

Strong leaders must agree to disagree at times with other professionals and parents in a kind and respectful manner. Listening, discussing, and collaboratively solving problems are necessary components of positive leadership skills. Holding themselves and others accountable for actions is one way to model leadership behavior. The same set of rules should be applied by the leader to him-/herself as expected of other adults in the school and community.

Maxwell (2010) discussed the importance of connecting when communicating with others. This key concept takes the term "effective communication" to the idea of words meaning nothing unless the receiver of those words not only understands the words said, but can truly understand what the words mean. For example, how a conversation makes a person feel should be a measure of effective communication.

Application of this can be demonstrated in a few ways. A principal leaves the following message on your answering machine: "Good afternoon. I really need to talk to you, so please call me back today." The parent immediately starts to worry what happened to their child, what did their child do that was a problem, what kind of trouble did their child get into in school today that warranted such a call? The well-intended principal left the message with the excitement of sharing a good thing the child did in school today and couldn't wait to inform the parent. Both responses were based on assumptions, but resulted in opposite feelings.

CHANGING SCHOOL CULTURE THROUGH COLLABORATION

People are typically resistant to change. Fear of the unknown, comfort levels, questioning why change matters happens in all systems when changes occur. It is important to recognize, address, and plan appropriately when you are the leader in a system or organization that is undergoing change.

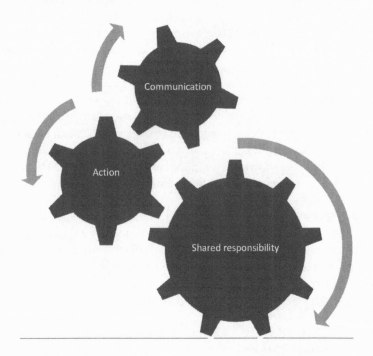

Figure 4.2.   Relationship between Communication and Action in Responsibility

Communication, transparency, and opportunities to discuss change with stakeholders provide a mechanism for stakeholders to deal with change. These attributes are also key points of building relationships and trust (Haines et al. 2015).

Price (2008) wrote about mobilizing communities to help students succeed. Both affective (feeling) and concrete (analyze) domains contribute to the support of change. Parents want their children to be in a safe learning environment, one that is welcoming of their input and demonstrates results. Parents and teachers feel good when children are happy and are able to demonstrate that they learned presented information. The analysis of data supports these successes, identifies weaknesses, and produces a cycle of informed decision making for building and district leaders. Both domains influence adult's thinking of what needs to be done, how it needs to be done, and what modifications to current programs are needed for successful student outcomes.

Developing an understanding of what the change involves, who is impacted by the change, how the changes are facilitated and by whom are important considerations when a new concept is presented to the school community. Effectively communicating with staff members, parents, and community groups is a critical component of leading organizational change.

Parents and school personnel become weary of continual change presented in school districts. Areas of non-sustainable change due in part to regulatory changes from the federal government (federal programs: Title 1; IDEA), state (assessment, curriculum requirements), district initiatives under ever-changing leadership create investments in time and resources that often are never fully actualized. Parental involvement is targeted in federal programs like Title 1 and special education funding (IDEA). However, those programs are limited to include certain groups of parents and do not meet the broader needs of all parents in a school community. In fact, those programs make it easy for district leaders to ensure compliance with those mandates, but not make changes to district policy and practice for all students and families.

Building a caring community of stakeholders in a sustainable parent, community, and school partnership requires creating ownership in each group. This necessitates the need for a commitment of time and resources from leadership (superintendent, board of education, community partners). Change takes time, and programs cannot achieve sustainability if they are dependent on a person. The need to build partnerships, create ownership, and develop values supporting the partnerships are required entities.

In order to accomplish this, district plans need to encourage, promote, and support these partnerships. Creating systems of shared responsibility for student achievement as measured by learning outcomes that include both school and families is critical for success (Weiss and Stephen 2009).

PARENT UNIVERSITY/ACADEMY CONCEPT

Engaging parents and guardians as partners to support student achievement is the primary goal of Parent University/Academy Programs (PUP/PAP). Parent University/Academy Programs are one way to create an important role for parents as partners in school settings. A PUP/PAP is a professional conference for parents by parents, facilitated by school personnel and supported by the community. Focus is on communication, collaboration, coordination, and celebration of working together for student success.

Key differences from other parent training programs include:

- District-wide planning and implementation
- Multithemed topics
- Building capacity of all stakeholders
- Student to student
- Parent to parent
- Staff members to students and parents
- Community involvement with students, parents, and school system
- Positive presentation of workshop material

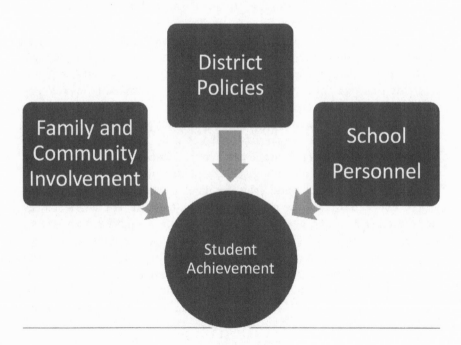

Figure 4.3.   Influences on Student Achievement

Parent University/Academy Programs are research based, and have begun appearing in many school districts across the country as well as in university and college programs. The program is developed for each community based on data gathered from survey results. Evaluation of the event is gathered from parents and guardians, presenters, students, and community participants.

An action-research model is followed in structuring a PUP. Data is gathered from stakeholders, a program is developed around topics identified, and feedback is collected and collated from participants and shared with stakeholders. The data is then used to plan the next PU/AP event and a similar process is followed.

Barnyak and McNelly (2009) identified the core components of an action plan for increased family involvement that should be based upon the six standards suggested by the National Parent Teacher Association. These include welcoming all families into the school community, communicating effectively, supporting student success, speaking up for every child, sharing power, and collaborating with the community.

Parent University/Academy Programs help a community to celebrate the partnership and values between school system leadership and stakeholders. In the past, schools contacted parents and guardians if a professional thought there was a problem that was evident. For example, if a child was acting out in school, parents may be told about a "parenting workshop" they could attend to learn how to "parent better." This approach was not only insulting to parents, but further separated relationships between school personnel and families. A negative value statement was made from a "something needs to be fixed" perspective.

Parent University/Academy programs reverse this trend. Asking parents what areas of school information they would like to learn more about (academics, college preparation, and student behavioral expectations) sends a message of collaboration on behalf of shared goals for students rather than a pinpoint of negative student issues or parental failures.

Parents and families want to be involved with their child(ren)'s school, but often lack the knowledge of how to be involved proactively. Therefore, it is a responsibility of the school district to invite, encourage, and assist parents and families in engaging productively in their child(ren)'s educational experience.

School events that involve student presentations often result in increased parent/family involvement. Coordinating musical presentations and student demonstrations are another way to engage participation in a PUP/PAP program. Sporting events create an additional opportunity to share this information, as many residents and family members attend.

COMMUNITY ENGAGEMENT

Many parents and family members of students work and live in the school community. Additionally, there are many who do not yet have children in the school or adults whose children have graduated. These community members are important contributors to the establishment of a collaborative effort to work with all stakeholders.

In some states, school budgets are voted upon each year. Adults who do not have children in the schools are voters. Their input matters. Instead of waiting for a reason to reach out to these constituents (problems, budget, and building projects) school leaders should encourage their participation in planning the PUP/PAP. Ask for their assistance throughout the steps outlined, as their history as parents or their fears and dreams of being parents of school-aged children will be of great value to the project and to the district.

Schools with limited time or funding to provide transportation or those that are located too far from museums and other similar organizations, might look at the reverse of place-based education and consider ways to bring the organizations on campus. Most museums and zoos have activities and arti-facts that can travel. Many can provide great ideas for parent and/or family nights.

One school in central Florida had struggled to get significant engagement of families for night events that focused on specific content. They were searching for a way to get families excited about math and science. They partnered with a local museum to create an interactive science night. It was so successful (more than doubled the expected attendance) that the following school year they partnered for both a science and a math night. More impor-tantly, the museum also provided experiences throughout the day for all of the students so that even if the student's family could not attend the evening event, they were still able to experience some of the museum activities. These activities were carefully chosen to support upcoming science and math units and they generated significant student enthusiasm for the topics/con-cepts presented.

A different school in the same district took a similar, but different ap-proach. The staff at this school knew that children from poverty lack experi-ences in the community that other students have. Looking for ways to level the playing field and build background knowledge, they also looked at the concept of place-based education and designed day-long experiences where the entire student body could explore facets of the community. Instead of taking the students out into the community, the community came into the school.

One day they focused on the theme of "our community" and students explored nineteen stations that were manned by different community mem-bers and their tools, equipment, or props. This ranged from the fire department to the SWAT team to a local grocery chain that provided a semi-truck for the kids to explore to an archaeological dig sponsored by a local university. The second day-long event concentrated more on the visual and performing arts and ranged from musical and drama performances from the local middle and high school to a team from a local dance company to a music store that provided instruments for the children to explore and to local artists who talked about their genre of art and what it takes to be a professional artist.

For each event, the entire school was involved and then teachers used the event as a springboard for an appropriate grade-level writing activity where the students could put their new vocabulary words to use. The music and art teachers also used the event as the introduction to a new unit and developed a research activity around the station exploration. Since the students had the opportunity to see, touch, or feel the items in the station, the vocabulary connections were greater.

Another approach concentrates on partnerships that assist with the transition from pre–K to kindergarten (Emfinger 2012). In her article, "Literacy Readiness: Transitional Partnerships between Preschool and Kindergarten," Emfinger discusses the success of the Deerfield Preschool Kindergarten Readiness Alliance. The providers in this alliance participated in articulation meetings with the kindergarten teachers and both pre–K and kindergarten teachers attended professional development together. Not only did it positively impact student achievement, but the articulation between teachers at the different grade levels improved.

One school in central Florida used a similar concept to grow transitional partnerships among pre–K providers, but then used the same concept to improve articulation between all of the grades at the elementary school and neighboring middle school. Imagine a school where each grade level team meets with the grade above and below it to talk about readiness and key entry level skills that students need to be successful at that grade. Teachers truly gained a deeper understanding of which set of standards and benchmarks are essential for students to master.

An unintended result was that teams not only became more vested in the learning gains, but they requested more opportunities for the teams to meet and they wanted to help with student placements for the following year. They were vested in the students beyond the year in their grade level. In addition, teams of teachers visited the classrooms in the grades below and above them to see teaching and learning in action. They had a chance to observe lessons and student activities and see the great ideas for both curriculum and classroom management. The sense of community and commitment to the success of each student and the school grew exponentially and the classroom visits were so well received that teachers requested the same opportunity the following year.

The power of parents as partners is undeniable. There is a large body of research that supports the existence of school parent partnerships and, from that, policies that range from Title 1 requirements to some teacher evaluation systems. According to Mapp and Kuttner (2013), most policies are based upon the assumption that parents and school staff know how to be effective partners, but that is far from the truth. One school with a high migrant population used a slightly different transitional model than the one described in the Deerfield alliance (Emfinger 2012).

The pre–K and kindergarten teams met with the migrant organization that provided pre–K services for many of the migrant children. Together, they designed a packet that the migrant families could take with them as they traveled up north. It had enough activities to last for the summer until they returned to Florida. These activities were designed so that the children would continue to develop some of the key academic skills they would need as they entered kindergarten. Keep in mind that these families leave Florida before the school year ends and return to Florida after the next year has started.

The partnership of teachers developed a parent training session that was provided at the migrant association that was delivered just before the families moved north. Many of the parents are illiterate in both English and Spanish so training was key if the packets were going to be used.

The most immediate result was that the parents saw that the teachers and the school wanted the children to be as successful as their parents did. Secondly, they appreciated that the teachers recognized that they would not know what to do with the activities if no one showed them, BUT that they were trusted to carry out the activities now that training had been provided. The hesitancy on the part of the migrant parents is understandable.

A similar hesitancy is noted with a pre–K readiness program in Farmington, New Mexico. In that program, the library system has been working to establish partnerships with their Hispanic and Navajo families. They discovered that many of the families were not confident moving within the educational system and had little knowledge of pre–K education (Celano and Neuman 2016). Building confidence through parent training is a win-win situation, indeed. This "win" is reinforced by many studies. In John Hattie's book, *Visible Learning* (2009), he states, "Parents should be taught the language of schooling so that the home and school can share expectations" (p. 70). He specifically highlights the results of a metaanalysis that focuses on parent involvement. Senechal (2006) found that a more active involvement by parents was more effective. For example, the effect size from studies where parents taught their children specific literacy skills were twice as effective (d = 1.15) as parents listening to their children read (d = 0.51) which, in turn, was more effective than reading to the child (d = 0.18)" (Hattie 2009, p. 70).

Community members can participate in school activities through a variety of means. Businesses in the local geographical area of the school/district are often asked to contribute money for special events. Surveying businesses and asking what relationship they desire with the school district, asking what resources they have to offer to students in clubs, courses, and determining what skill sets in graduates they look for as employers are proactive and positive ways of engaging members of the community. If a business owner is vested in the community, the school district is a vital part of that community, and shared communication benefits businesses, school district, students, and the community.

Senior citizens are another group of individuals in every community and should be encouraged to participate in school events. Schools often offer local senior citizens free tickets to musical events (plays, concerts) and through the PUP/PAP, another role for senior citizens emerge. Their expertise from career paths, volunteerism, knowledge of children and the community, and the desire to be active participants in events should be solicited in planning a PUP/PAP event.

Inviting parents of preschool students in programs in the district taps into parents of future students in a proactive, positive manner. During kindergarten registration events, sharing information about the Parent Involvement Committee and PUP/PAP program also entices parents who are often looking for ways to "enter" the school system with their children and get involved.

In most communities, there are street fairs, parades, races, and other events that celebrate the local opportunities for residents. These are also places where sharing information about an upcoming PUP/PAP event or inviting others to participate in planning such an event is a worthwhile endeavor. A simple flyer can be distributed announcing the opportunities.

Engaging all constituents requires a commitment of time, leadership, facilitation, and a strategic plan that is developed and implemented with input from representatives of various groups: teachers, administrators, parents, community members, students, and support staff. Communicating within the school community and with community stakeholders is the most important aspect of building a district-wide, successful parental partnership. In order to initiate a successful program, trustful relationships must be created so that there is a framework for ongoing program success based on parental needs.

PARENT INVOLVEMENT TASK FORCES: PARTNERS IN CRITICAL ANALYSIS AND PLANNING

In New York, one district investigated how to engage families positively. The exploration of parent involvement took several months and generated lengthy discussions that clearly uncovered the complexity of cooperative inquiry and the intricacies of a topic as seemingly simple as parent involvement. The group was surprised by their own discourse and discoveries not only about the topic but about each other. They moved the question of how to improve parental involvement to the question of knowing what issues were most important to parents with respect to their child's education.

Several guided discussions helped to develop categories of inquiry. The categories covered a wide range of topics such as communication between school officials and parents, communication between teacher and parents, student homework, student safety concerns, school volunteers, parent availability for school meetings, parenting skill development, student transitions from elementary to middle to high school, preparation for college and career choices, managing adolescent behaviors, test preparations, reading instruction at home, special education, and access to technology.

This committee did return to its original question about improving parent involvement but with a deeper understanding of the topic. Their discussions led to clearer ideas on what they wanted to accomplish and how to elicit further information from parents, the school faculty, and other community members. In this particular case, the members of the committee, parents and school leaders together, developed a survey that retrieved vital information that was then shared with the district for decision making.

The survey questions were developed directly from the inquiry categories noted above. Not only did the group create the survey, but through their inquiry they determined how best to implement and conduct the survey in order to reach more parents and in order to obtain a substantial response rate from survey participants.

The data gathered from the survey helped to define the changing needs and interests of parents as their children moved from elementary to middle to high school. The results influenced the school district so strongly that a parent conference was conducted that spoke directly to the topics and results of the survey.

Subsequently, a parent conference program, or Parent University Program, was established and became a biannual event for the school district. Response to the event was spectacular and dramatically increased parent involvement in a variety of ways. A unique by-product of this participatory action research (PAR) was that two of the original committee members subsequently obtained seats on the board of education.

So, why was this example of participatory action research seemingly successful? What are the factors that helped to make it successful? Let's examine some of the key factors.

First of all, a key element that was operating in this particular example was the makeup of the group. Who were the members of the inquiry team that would be asking the questions and creating the potential answers? In this case, the group was made up of members of teachers, school administrators, and parents.

A cross section membership of the school community sphere is important to the entire process and subsequent outcomes of a PAR. If this had been an inquiry group consisting of only teachers or only parents, the discourse and the subsequent actions would have been entirely different and most likely would have resulted in low impact or ineffective actions. On the other hand, the diversity of this group guaranteed that the work and results would not be measured or defined as only by one group/role, but would be more representative of parents, administrators, and school personnel.

The question needs to be raised as to whether these particular members adequately represented the "school-parent" community. Upon closer examination, the committee which was addressing parent involvement, had parent members that by their very presence were already "involved." They did not necessarily represent the uninvolved parent.

In addition, the parents on the committee were not necessarily representative of the socioeconomically disadvantaged families in the community, which in this particular district constituted a large portion of the school community. Indeed, this non-representation factor had the potential to deprive the group of the capacity for honest inquiry and therefore create biased and perhaps ineffective outcomes.

This is a common obstacle in many school-community committees that struggle to get representative constituency for discussion and shared decision making processes. But, it does not have to be an absolute deterrent to discourse and action.

Administrators and school leaders do need to recognize this as a potential problem but they need also to move ahead committed to their objectives and purpose. According to social change theorists, organizing leaders will always be in the process of defining and broadening the constituency base (Fisher 1994).

The same was true for the school representatives on this committee. Most were district and building administrators with only two middle school level teachers represented. This committee did well to recognize who was not represented. They reached out for other teacher members from the elementary schools and high school and included new members as tasks were generated and as the conference event was being planned. Likewise, more and more parents and local community members joined as the surveys were conducted and the subsequent parent conference was designed and implemented.

In other words, the practice of building a representative constituency base was ongoing and expanded as the committee defined its tasks and recruited new members. Although the committee started out with constituency gaps, it committed itself to filling those gaps and addressing its need for representative members.

A second important factor is the leadership of the committee. In this case, the leaders who were school administrators had previous experience in developing parent-school groups and clearly understood the process and means for developing partnerships between school personnel and parent members. The key ingredient was that the committee leaders had a solid understanding of the degrees and levels of partnership needed.

According to Nelson and Guerra (2010), there are three levels of school-family partnerships: family involvement, family engagement, and family empowerment. Family involvement is a fairly individualized type of parental connection, focusing mostly on how parents can connect with their own child's education through home and school activities.

Family engagement brings the parent into a role of working with the school to affect and focus on broad based school activities. Family empowerment occurs when parents/families work together as equal partners to effect change through shared resources, information, and decision making. Family empowerment is qualitatively different from involvement and engagement in that the inherent power of school authorities is shared, that school practices are transparent, and parents are given key information and access to the school.

In the case described here, the committee leaders were operating on all three levels but were primarily focused on family engagement. The objective of the committee was to increase parental involvement. Based on the committee's discourse, they clearly determined that more information was needed from district families regarding the core notion of parental involvement. This led to the development of a survey. The survey itself offered questions about family involvement and suggested ways to generate family engagement. The third level, namely family empowerment, became an implicit opportunity through the use of the survey in designing and implementing the parent conference and the subsequent parent university event.

The management of family empowerment is a skill that would require consistent school/district leadership and the support of the local school board of education. It is the development, construction, implementation, and analysis of a survey that offers the best and easiest means for engaging parent and school personnel together. The participation together (survey) creates action (parent conference) through the use of research (survey results).

The third element is that research through participation greatly assisted and augmented parental involvement. The very act of asking parents to contribute questions about keys areas of interest such as homework, adolescent behavior, school communications, and career and college preparation generated more contacts and conversations with parents. And consequently, more families began to join the effort. As questions were designed for the survey, deeper insights into the understanding of parent involvement emerged. In fact, this process helped to bust some typical myths about parent involvement. At the start of the committee's work, for example, there was a belief that the ideal time for parents to meet with teachers was during after-school hours.

This notion was challenged repeatedly when it was revealed that many parents preferred school time hours and some preferred Saturday morning hours. Of course, much of this feedback revealed the diverse pressures and effects of single parent households, unemployed family members, and those that were doubly employed family members. It also demonstrated that in a diverse community, there will be diverse preferences regarding school involvement.

PAR activity was able to assist in addressing notions and beliefs of school personnel about parents that tended to perpetuate parent-school gaps. In a study by Hindin (2010), student teachers were interviewed during their field studies in urban school settings indicating that they did not observe ideal interactions between families and teachers.

Less than positive perceptions by urban school teachers about parents played a role in the transmission of information to the student teacher, thus contributing to the cycle of potential negative misperceptions about urban parents' involvement in their child's school. It is extremely important that school leaders understand the economic and cultural diversity issues within their local community in order to guide school-parent groups in a PAR project.

In the case example of our Shared Decision Making Committee, an unspoken but implied myth that was detected was that parents do not get involved with their child's school because the parent doesn't care or that the parent is lazy or that the parent has lingering negative experiences from their own childhood school experiences. As the research group began analyzing their data and qualitatively weighing their conversations with parents, the group quickly realized that social and economic factors along with the difficulties of raising children in a single parent household were more likely to be reasonable sources for the lack of parent involvement.

The survey also indicated clearly that parent preferences and teacher expectations for parent involvement changed over time or as their students moved from elementary to secondary levels of school. The first draft of the survey did not provide differentiation of parents' responses according to the school and grade levels of their children. Preliminary conversations with parents and feedback from PTSO and PTA groups suggested that the concerns of families with children in elementary schools were uniquely different from those with children in middle and high school. As a result, the survey was changed to account for these differences thus enriching the value of the data.

When the results were gathered, the group was able to analyze data according to grade levels and individual schools. This was a simple adjustment that yielded greater meaning in the final data. Another part of the survey revealed that many parents had children enrolled on all three levels at the same time, creating very real obstacles for parental participation in school meetings and activities.

The final element of productive and effective PAR is whether there is a conscious effort to sustain the action, the results, and the process of the research. Sustainability of parent school partnerships takes dedication to dialogue, willingness to share authority with each other (school and parents), and a commitment to community revitalization (Auerbach 2007). Participatory Action Research provides a meaningful vehicle for engaging parents and families with school personnel, for challenging and sharing beliefs and goals, and for strengthening those partnerships with measured information that can shape school policy and practices.

There is no doubt that any school leader who takes on the responsibility for PAR must have some knowledge and training in the area of developing groups and in the area of basic research. Most college programs for school administration promote the use of research in creating educational papers and theses but there is not a strong enough emphasis on research methodology and practice in using research "with" constituents.

Although this text does not address the specifics of research theory and practice, it does encourage school leaders to have a working knowledge of basic survey research methods as well as the overlapping requirements of naturalistic inquiry, qualitative study, and more conventional quantitative research. And yet, in stating this, it is important to remember that for our purposes, the act of research begins with the very simple task of bringing people (teachers, community members, and parents) together as members of a school community with a hope to create change. For the methods of survey research, it is always helpful for school leaders to identify and engage research experts for guidance and consultation.

In his ground breaking book, *The Fifth Discipline* (1990), Peter Senge speaks about the art of creating conversations among groups and individuals within learning organizations. What better learning organization is there than a school community? Senge claims that dialogue is a critical component of the process of partnership and team building. It takes place through the use of conversation. Dialogue fosters positive interaction and exchange of new ideas between school leaders, families, and community members. It helps to bridge the gaps that typically and counterdynamically thwart connections between schools, families, and communities.

Dialogue is uniquely different from discussion and must be understood by school leaders as part of their role in the school-parent-community triumvirate. Dialogue is a process that enables a group to develop new views on specific issues. Discussion also provides opportunities for participants to share thoughts and ideas but it does not necessarily lead to the development of new ideas and actions. The school leader will be challenged to balance the discussions and dialogue process so that ideas can be generated and actions can be implemented.

According to Bohm (1965), there are three conditions that are required for dialogue to occur. The first requirement asks participants to "suspend" their notions or thoughts about the other entities or members of the larger group. These notions may include parents who think that teachers and schools communicate poorly, or that the school just doesn't care as well as school personnel who feel that parents are not involved enough in their child's education or that the parents are more likely to complain than to complement the school system. It may also include community members who feel that the school is not doing a good enough job or that the parents are not raising their children with proper values. In the process of establishing positive interactions and conversations, each group is asked to hold off on those notions and leave room for new and additional thoughts regarding the school system, parenting, and community support.

The second requirement asks all participants to view each other as colleagues. This seems like a contradictory task for school leaders who are inherently relied upon by teachers, parents, and themselves as the holders of authority in the school community. It is no less difficult for parents who serve as authorities in their own right at home for their children and other members of the family to view a school leader as a colleague. Community members also wear various mantels of authority in their daily lives and businesses that then have to be hung up to engage in meaningful and positive dialogue with community partners such as schools and parents.

A greeting phrase that welcomes participants to school family meetings in our current school is "leave your axes at the door and get ready to work in peace." An example of the idea of collegiality is a group that the author started for parents of students on the autism spectrum. At first, the author, as school leader, was responsible for all invitations, setting the agenda, copying all materials, creating mailing lists, bringing the food, making the coffee, conducting the meeting and follow-up minutes of the meeting.

The initial meetings focused on purposes, goals, and recruitment of members. Once that was established and participants felt that the format was set, the "suspended assumptions" emerged. And yes, there were some tenuous moments that had the potential to put various factions on the defensive. From my perspective, however, the group was beginning to feel comfortable enough to share their notions without fear of reprisal. A level of trust was building. Having developed groups and partnerships before, I knew that this part of the journey toward a trusting partnership was inevitable and necessary for true and meaningful dialogue. An untrained school leader might fear at this point that the group will get out of hand and rebel. However, the pattern of group development (Stewart and Shamdasani 1990) indicates that groups can storm just after they form and right before they norm.

The authority dilemma also follows some positive and predictable patterns. Toward the sixth or seventh meeting of the parent autism group, the agenda began to be created by the members rather than the school leader. Invitations to meetings were transferred to various parent members. One parent donated a free website through his company along with technology assistance. Members began to share responsibilities for food and coffee. The facilitator struggled to not sit at the head of the table and share that position with school leaders and parent members.

Persistently, the group still turns to the school leaders when dialogue gets stuck. However, the reclaiming of the leadership role by the school leader can be momentary and effective if handled as a facilitator rather than a chairperson or a director. This lingering role of responsibility explains the third requirement for positive dialogue.

When developing school-family-community partnerships, it is usually the case that the school leader serves as the initiator for partnership. There are a few exceptions when parent groups or community organizations take the lead role in effecting partnerships with schools, such as with the development of charter schools or to create changes that affect the safety and welfare of students in challenging neighborhoods in which the school is located. In either case, there is always a need for someone to serve as the facilitator and driver for the dialogues that are needed.

Do not be misled into thinking that the school leader develops a parent group to the point that the school leader is no longer needed. The school leader can never divest herself of the responsibility of building school-parent-community partnerships. The school leader has the predesignated responsibility not only to promote and develop school-parent partnerships but to support its sustainability over time.

Establishing a culture of collaboration allows for parents and school faculty to work together successfully. Developing ownership of an ongoing Parent University Program in order to create sustainability of the program is an important component.

Parent University Program workshops should include presentations by district staff across buildings and disciplines. This collaborative model allows for parents to learn about curriculum, standards, behavioral expectations that encompass expectations for all students. Supporting faculty in working together to present workshop topics identified by survey results builds community capacity for parents. This supports the relationships parents have with individual teachers and schools, and identifies how those smaller pieces fit into the larger district goals and expectations.

Teachers and faculty benefit from having the opportunity to work with colleagues in developing workshops. For example, if a workshop presentation is focused on a primary school (grades pre-K–2) issue such as learning through play, teachers from all schools with children in this age range should work across school boundaries to present workshops. It is very powerful when parents hear that what is being offered in their child's classroom is the same as others in the district, and listening to their own child's teacher's expertise is impressive as ways to have parents learn how to be supportive of school activities.

Additionally, when school personnel hear parent input, questions, and comments, it assists teachers in learning what they may need to do differently to ensure parental understanding, reinforces their knowledge as they share ideas and learn from colleagues, and validates much of the work that is done in the classroom. Teaching is often an isolated activity, as children work in a classroom with one teacher per day or per period. Traditionally, schools do not support content or grade level team coordination between schools, as it is difficult to accomplish that in each school due to time restraints.

The interdependence of these three groups significantly impacts student expectation and performance. While students need to take responsibility for themselves as students, how schools assist parents and family members in supporting and nurturing their children toward meeting shared goals is the basis of a sustainable PUP/PAP. Hendersen and Mapp (2002) specified that parents recognize positive interactions as those tied to their children's learning. Improvements in student achievement were noted when families were engaged in supporting their children's learning at home, over a period of time, and recognized variations in income levels, education, and cultural backgrounds.

Successful programs are centered on connecting families, school staff, and community members in developing trustful and respectful relationships that are built on mutual understanding, welcoming opportunities, and organized programs. Henderson et al. (2007) described essential guides to successful school-family partnerships. Many of their points are those discussed in earlier chapters, including how to encourage both school-based and district support of strong parent involvement in schools. A parent may receive a request to bake something for a PTA/PTO fundraiser for their child's school. This is a seemingly easy request to fulfill, and items are sent to the school to be sold. This is an example of a "one-shot event" where parents feel connected and helpful.

However, how do we systemically develop this level of support into a comprehensive cycle of sharing responsibility, power, and engagement of parents and the school community? School leaders must recognize that schools and students' homes are not isolated from one another. Rather, leaders must acknowledge how schools can utilize the interconnections of students, families, and community in building productive partnerships that collaboratively support student success. The National Parent Teacher Associa-

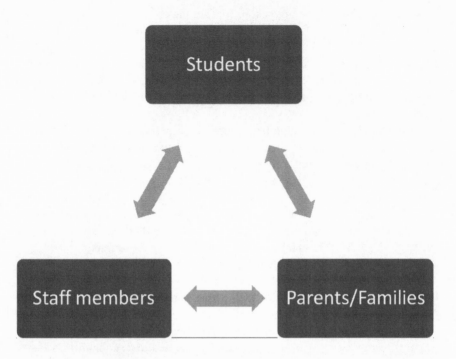

Figure 4.4. Visualization of Teaching Engagements

tion developed six national standards for parent involvement that have been the basis for much work in developing family-school-community partnerships (Barnyak and McNelly 2009). They include welcoming connected students to the community through expanded learning opportunities for students. All people want to be acknowledged for their contribution to an event and adding significance to other's work is an important concept that contributes to sustainability (Maxwell 1997). Valuing family differences and communicating with families across cultures is extremely important all families into the school community, communicating effectively, supporting student success, speaking to every child, sharing power, and collaborating with the community (National PTA 1997).

Parents and families need to feel and be welcomed, valued, and connected through their child, have meaningful two-way conversations about student learning and challenges, be able to collaborate and celebrate their student and collective student success, be empowered to be advocates for their children, have the ability to share input that impacts policies, practices, and programs for students, and have a defined and respected role (Allen 2007; Eberly, Joshi, and Konzal 2007).

Recognition that many parents have had negative interactions with schools is vital to planning and executing a successful parent involvement program. Parents represent many different students including students with high levels of achievement, struggling learners, students with disabilities, ELL/ESL learners, students who have been suspended, etc. School leaders must recognize all of these and talk honestly with parents and then sustain commonalities that bridge differences to work together as a school community.

It is important for leaders, both community and school, to share history in the community so that well-intended facilitators understand previous challenges in the district. In one district where I was the superintendent, I questioned why there was no district-wide parent group, and just started one with the assistance of building principals. I did not know that a previous superintendent had stopped the practice, as he/she did not encourage parent involvement in the schools and considered this a type of group interference in district operations, rather than a partnership of support.

There needs to be a systemic approach to sustainability of successful PUP/PAP programs. A district policy that supports and recognizes the value of school community involvement is an important step for the school system (Westmoreland et al. 2009). Policies are meant to provide the framework for the work that is done by the school district. If importance is placed on developing and implementing policies that support a parent involvement committee, stating who the members are, how they are solicited each year, representative of all school district students (including those parents whose students attend other schools, such as private, parochial, or special education programs located outside of the district buildings), the policy will assist sustainability of the value the district places on school-parent-community involvement. A policy can also be developed that specifies the district role in hosting a PUP/PAP each year and the roles and responsibility of the school facilitator.

Creating a systemic, sustainable parent/family involvement program in a school community that supports positive student outcomes is an enormous undertaking. As described in chapters 1–4, there are many variables that must be considered by the school district, including leadership, organizational goals, BOE policy, shared responsibility and ownership, commitment of resources and continuity, connection, and communication.

In order to build and sustain parent programs, parents must be engaged in the creation, implementation, and evaluation of PUP/PAP programs. If an action plan was developed for implementation, a second action plan should be developed for sustainability.

One aspect of a sustainable system is to create a strategic plan for the school community. The Harvard Research Project (2010) identified three major considerations for sustainable family engagement: shared responsibility; continuity across the grades from early childhood through high school graduation; and carried out in multiple settings where students learn. The team from Harvard suggested, based on a significant body of research, that families play a significant role in supporting student learning in schools, homes, and community.

The strategic plan must involve the Parent Involvement Committee, and roles for all sharing responsibility must be defined, articulated clearly, agreed upon, and acted upon. Families state they want to be involved; school personnel must describe how parents can be involved through activities and an action plan.

Darch, Miao, and Shippen (2004) summarized four categories for the implementation of a successful parent involvement program. Programs need to be proactive and encourage positive interactions with parents in a variety of ways throughout the school year. An action plan should be added for the school year (180 days); schools should inform parents of shared activities; and accommodations should be made to meet the needs of families of diverse backgrounds, work schedules, and resources.

One way to keep Parent Involvement Committee (PIC) members involved in a year-long process is for families to create portfolios. Typically, school calendars include monthly notification of building events (family math nights, family fun nights, open houses, parent–teacher conferences). In order to have PIC members assist in the cyclic delivery of PUP/PAP, at the first meeting of the year data from the prior year's PUP/PAP should be shared. Then, each family should start creating a family portfolio, collecting artifacts from their own family's involvement which can be shared at subsequent PIC meetings.

While this group develops a survey for parents each year, collects data, reviews parental interests, and plans the next PUP/PAP, they are engaged in putting together their own portfolio which will help them determine gaps in the parental involvement program in the district. Portfolios should be developed as an introduction to the process of gathering data for the PIC.

Each district should have a Parent Involvement Policy. While policy manuals and associated regulations are required documents, they are often "shelf art" rather than a working document. Policy manuals are requirements that are often completed and updated in order to meet regulations, rather than useful tools that assist in the effective management of the school district.

The PIC can have a leadership role in effectively engaging parents from policy to practice that increases sustainability of parent involvement in a district. The PIC can help identify, through their work on the PUP/PAP, aspects of parental involvement that is research-based, collaborative, and successful for that district. Memorializing annual PUP/PAP programs in a policy would be a critical support for sustainability. The policy can indicate what concept is and specify how it will be funded, and the administrative regulations can indicate who from the school district's administrative team (position) will facilitate the program and how it will be funded.

Each school and district leader should have a role in the implementation of the PIC and PUP/PAP. Building leader's facilitation of their PTA/PTO's involvement in the PIC and PUP/PAP is an important aspect of sustainable involvement. Recognition of their role should be supported by district leaders, and communication about the process, meetings, and programs should be provided by the district facilitator of the PIC and PUP/PAP teams. It is very important to communicate activities with all district leaders so that all stakeholders have an opportunity for communicating to/from the planning committee.

As mentioned in earlier chapters, communication is extremely important throughout the planning stages and implementation of a successful and sustainable PUP/PAP program. The cycle of effective communication is a key to keeping constituents engaged in the activities of researching, implementing, and evaluating the program.

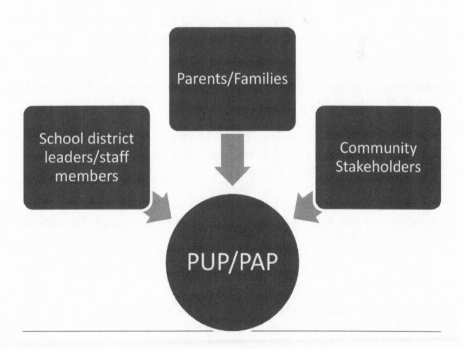

Figure 4.5.   Communication Flowchart in Education

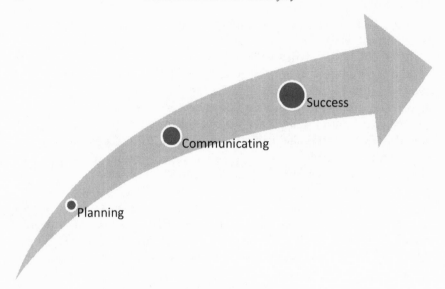

Figure 4.6.   Cycle of Effective Communication

LEADERSHIP DEVELOPMENT

Leaders emerge from family members, teachers, students, and administrators throughout the process of engaging families. School systems that invite parents and families to participate in collaborative efforts with school staff enable students to increase their success. Partnerships that focus on proactive engagement of parents and families significantly increase support for district, school, and students.

A PUP/PAP Program facilitates this positive relationship between school and families. While each community or district's program may look different, the PUP/PAP development process tailors the program to meet individual system's needs, engages local community members into the process, and enables relationships within the school system and between the school system and community to be developed, nurtured, and sustained.

When schools and parents work together, students always benefit. At both the university and K–12 setting, leaders are developed in all stakeholder groups through various partnerships as described.

KEY IDEAS IN THIS CHAPTER

- Family engagement at university and K–12 schools
- Impact of family engagement
- Leaders emerge from partnerships with families

• Changing culture requires transparency and communication with and between all stakeholders

SUMMARY

The importance of recognizing families as critical partners in both the university and K–12 settings is well supported in K–12 research, but minimally identified in university programs. Looking at a cross section of research from different perspectives, the engagement of families and students helps all organizations sustain faculty, students, programs of studies, and supports educational and business partnerships by meeting their needs of IHE graduates. It is difficult to build leadership capacity of students, faculty, and other members of the community if students and faculty do not remain in one location. Recognition of the importance of engagement to support students, faculty, and organizations through family engagement is a benefit to all, especially as students demonstrate success.

1. **During this school year, how well has your child's school been doing the following things?**

(MARK ONE RESPONSE ON EACH LINE)

	Not well at all	Not well	Well	Very well	I Don't know
a. Lets you know between report cards how your child is doing in school?	○	○	○	○	○
b. Helps you understand what children at your child's age are like?	○	○	○	○	○
c. Makes you aware of chances to volunteer at the school?	○	○	○	○	○
d. Provides workshops, materials, or advice about how to help your child learn at home?	○	○	○	○	○
e. Provides information on community services to help your child or your family?	○	○	○	○	○
f. Provides information about how to help your child with his/her homework?	○	○	○	○	○
g. Provides information about why your child is placed in particular groups or classes?	○	○	○	○	○
h. Provides information on how to help your child plan for college or vocational school?	○	○	○	○	○
i. Provides information about how to help your child plan for work after he/she completed his/her education?	○	○	○	○	○
j. Provides opportunities for you to have a say in policy decisions?	○	○	○	○	○

2. **How satisfied are you with...**

(MARK ONE RESPONSE ON EACH LINE)

	Very dissatisfied	Somewhat dissatisfied	Somewhat satisfied	Very satisfied
a. the school your child attends this year?	○	○	○	○
b. the teachers your child has this year?	○	○	○	○
c. the academic standards of the school?	○	○	○	○

Figure 4.7.   Family Involvement and Engagement Survey

d. the order and discipline at the school?   ○   ○   ○   ○

3   Have any of your child's teachers or his/her school contacted you about any <u>behavior</u> problems he/she is having in school this year?

○ Yes   ○ No

4   Have any of your child's teachers or his/her school contacted you about any problems he/she is having with <u>school work</u> this year?

○ Yes   ○ No

5   Since the beginning of the school year, have you or other adults in your household...

(list other parent events relevant to local school or district)   **(MARK ONE RESPONSE ON EACH LINE)**

	Yes	No	N/A
a. attended a general meeting, for example, an open house, a back-to-school night or a meeting of a parent-teacher organization?	○	○	○
b. gone to a regularly scheduled parent-teacher conference with your child's teacher?	○	○	○
c. attended a school or class event, such as a play, sports event, or science fair because of your child?	○	○	○
d. acted as a volunteer at the school or served on a committee?	○	○	○
e. served as a volunteer in the child's classroom?	○	○	○
f. participated in fundraising for the school?	○	○	○

6   **This year, about how much time *per week* does your child spend studying or doing homework for *ALL* of his/her classes?**

○ 2 hours or less per week   ○ 6 - 9 hours per week
○ 3 - 5 hours per week   ○ 10 or more hours per week

7   How do you feel about the amount of homework your child is assigned?

○ The amount is about right.   ○ It's too much.   ○ It's too little.

8   Is there a place in your home that is set aside for him/her to do homework?

○ Yes
○ No
○ Child does not do homework at home

Family Involvement and Engagement Survey

9   Do you or another adult in your household check to see that his/her homework is done?

o   Yes   o   No

10   How much do you agree or disagree with each of the following statements about the school your child attends?

(MARK ONE RESPONSE ON EACH LINE)

	Strongly agree	Agree	Disagree	Strongly disagree
a. When you walk into the school building it looks welcoming.	o	o	o	o
b. I feel welcome in this school.	o	o	o	o
c. In my child's school, everyone has the same opportunity to get good grades.	o	o	o	o
d. My child gets treated fairly by his/her teachers.	o	o	o	o
e. The punishment for breaking school rules is the same no matter who you are.	o	o	o	o
f. Everyone gets along in my child's school.	o	o	o	o
g. Students often get into physical fights on school grounds.	o	o	o	o
h. My child feels safe at their school.	o	o	o	o

11   As things stand now, how far in school do you think your child will get?

(MARK ONE RESPONSE)

o   Less than high school graduation

o   High school graduation or GED only

o   Attend or complete a 2-year school course in a community or vocational school

o   Attend college, but not complete a 4-year degree

o   Graduate from college

o   Obtain a Master's degree or equivalent

o   Obtain a Ph.D., M.D., or other advanced degree

o   Don't know

12   What do you feel are the main challenges parents experience in trying to communicate with the district?

Family Involvement and Engagement Survey (continued)

13   What are some effective communication strategies the district personnel can use to communicate with you?

14   Please provide one suggestion on how you think the district can improve your experience and

> In this section, we will ask you a few questions about yourself, your child and your background. This information will be used for comparison purposes only.

15   **What is your relationship to this child?**

o   Parent   o   Aunt or Uncle

o   Grandparent   o   Sibling

o   Legal Guardian   o   Other (please describe)

16   **What is your child's gender?**   o   Male   o   Female

17   **What grade is he/she in?**   _____

18   **Do you have any other children enrolled in the School District?**   _____

o   No

o   Yes. If Yes, how many other children do you have in the School District?   _____

19   **What is your gender?**   o   Male   o   Female

20   **Which of the following best describe the type of family that your child currently lives in?**

Family Involvement and Engagement Survey (continued)

o   Family is headed by a single parent/guardian

o   Family is headed by two parents/guardians

o   Family is headed by more than two parents/guardians (including extended family members)

o   Family is headed by a non-family member (including foster care and other child services placements)

Thank you for participating in our survey.

Overall findings will be made available to you by your school when ready.

- **This survey was created by the Hudson City School District Parent Involvement Committee and NYU (2007)**

Family Involvement and Engagement Survey (continued)

Chapter Five

Partnerships and Collaboration for Individuals with Disabilities

Denise Skarbek and Karen Hahn

The purpose of this chapter is to examine the K–16+ special education collaborative partnerships that have positive impacts on an individual with disabilities' education. This chapter is divided into two sections. The first section covers the K–12 level and the second section covers the university level (13–16+).

Both sections define collaboration as it relates to establishing partnerships with major stakeholders. Stages of collaboration (informing, involving, engaging, and leading as proposed by Hedeen, Moses, and Peter, n.d.) are defined and considered throughout the chapter when discussing collaborative partnerships. In addition, legislation that mandates collaboration for each level will be briefly reviewed and discussed.

Another area of focus at both the K–12 and university level is building capacity of leaders through collaboration with and for students with disabilities. There are great opportunities that can be fostered in program development, student centered support, and interagency collaboration.

All major stakeholders from K–16+ levels including school administrators, teachers, and parents of children with disabilities need to be collaboratively involved in the education of children with disabilities. In fact, the Individuals with Disabilities Act (IDEA) mandates active participation from major stakeholders in the individualized education planning process in the K–12 grades.

COLLABORATION

Each section provides recommendations on how to establish the collaborative partnerships at the respective levels. It should be noted that the authors assume collaboration must cascade and flow throughout all levels and is not an isolated act between K–12 and university levels.

Increasingly, it is evident that a cascade of collaboration is needed for an individual with disabilities beginning at birth and continuing throughout the individual's life span with all major stakeholders establishing partnerships. For the purposes of this chapter, we are only focusing at the K–16+ level and the partnerships between and within families, teachers, and communities. Each of these major stakeholders need to work closely together to meet the needs of individuals with disabilities.

Daniel (2011) describes two major theoretical underpinnings of family-school collaborative partnerships which serves as the foundation of collaborative partnerships at all levels. The theorists are Joyce Epstein and Urie Bronfenbrenner. Both theorists postulate a relationship between home-school-community for the development of the child. For our purposes, the child is considered to be an individual with disabilities.

Epstein (as cited in Daniel 2011) asserts the greater the relationship between the home, school, and community the greater the learning support for the child. Epstein's framework on parental involvement includes collaboration as one of the six types of supports needed by the family. By collaborating with the community, families acquire the needed resources and this ultimately leads to increased family participation.

Similarly, Bronfenbrenner's ecological model recognizes the interactions and collaborative relationships between the home, school, and community.

Daniel describes Bronfenbrenner's ecological model (as cited in Daniel, 2011) of human development. This theory proposes four levels of interaction: microsystem, mesosystem, exosystem, and macrosystem. Bronfenbrenner (as cited in Daniel 2011) suggested that these levels of interaction were a nested structure (see Figure 5.1). The inner circle is the microsystem which consists of the interaction of the biology of the child within the immediate environment.

Examples of these interactions include child-parent or child-teacher relationships. These relationships are bidirectional in that both the child and the adult are impacted. It is these interactions (proximal processes) that impact development. The next circle in the model is the mesosystem.

The mesosystem provides structure for the microsystem to intersect and consists of the home, school, and community interaction. An example of this is how well a child does in school is not only dependent on how well the child functions in the classroom but also on the support of his parents in these academic activities at home (Daniel 2011). It is within these two levels that

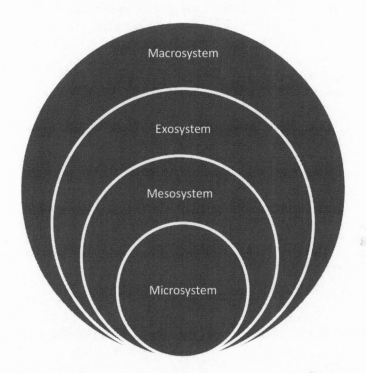

Figure 5.1.   Ecological Model for Cascade of Collaboration Partnerships for Individuals with Disabilities

linkages and processes takeplace between two or more settings containing an individual with disabilities in the micro and mesosystem that our collaborative partnerships focus on.

In addition, the teacher-teacher collaborative relationships at the K–12 level are also considered since this partnership has potential to positively impact on students with disabilities learning. An example of this is co-teaching.

LEGISLATION/POLICY

Family-school-community collaborative partnerships are supported with The Individuals with Disabilities Education Act (P.L. 105–17) legislation which mandates the involvement of parents in all decision making of children with disabilities. The Individuals with Disabilities Education Act ensures services for students with disabilities from birth to twenty-one years of age. This law entitles students with disabilities to a free, appropriate public education.

Students with certain disabilities in postsecondary education such as attention deficit hyperactivity disorder may be eligible for services under Section 504 of the Rehabilitation Act. This law provides a different level of services and support for students. The following is a review of legislation as it relates to collaboration at the postsecondary level.

Students attending a public or private institution are protected under Section 504 of the Rehabilitation Act (1973) and/or the Americans with Disabilities Act (ADA) (1990). Section 504 protects the rights of qualified individuals with disabilities from discrimination or participation in any program or event that receives funding from the government (epa.gov). The ADA prevents discrimination on the basis of a disability. The ADA defines an individual with a disability

> as a person who has a physical or mental impairment that substantially limits one or more major life activities, a person who has a history or record of such an impairment, or a person who is perceived by others as having such an impairment. (USDOJ 2009, para. 2)

One of the major differences between the protection under IDEA and Section 504 and the ADA is the increased responsibility on the individual student.

The student is required to request accommodations based on the documentation and request a letter be sent to specific courses each semester. While IDEA focuses on providing quality support, ADA and Section 504 focus on providing equal access and providing a level playing field for the student.

This tends to change the nature of the support a postsecondary student receives. The student is now responsible to build the partnerships and access the services provided by various agencies.

STAGES OF COLLABORATION

Informing is the least effective form of collaboration between students with disabilities, parents, and schools since this is a one-way form of communication. This is where the school sends communications to parents and students rather than a two-way form of communication.

Involving provides the agenda to parents and community members; whereas, *engaging* assumes that parents and community members create the agenda, make decisions together, and take actions. *Leading* occurs when parents, community members, and schools establish partnerships with appropriate leadership roles and all have common goals for shared vision and goals.

K–12 COLLABORATION

Some researchers (e.g., Cook and Friend 1995) espouse the need for collaboration for individuals with disabilities' education at the K–12 level especially between teachers who instruct children with disabilities. Collaboration is defined as, "two or more individuals working together towards a common goal of planning, implementing, or evaluating a specific aspect of an educational program for a student or group of students" (The IRIS Center for Training Enhancements 2007, p. 3).

The roles and responsibilities of general and special education teachers have changed. Teachers can no longer work in an isolated fashion thinking and in a silo. Collaboration is a way for teachers to share ideas and critically reflect on their classroom practice when working with students with disabilities. One common form known in the K–12 level is co-teaching for teacher-to-teacher partnerships.

Co-teaching, according to Cook and Friend (1995), is defined as "an approach where two professionals deliver substantive instruction to a group of students within a single physical space" (p. 1). Interestingly, Cook and Friend characterize co-teaching as an approach rather than a style of teaching. The partnerships of two people instructing individuals with disabilities provides more resources.

Teacher education programs are using the co-teaching approach during student teaching placements. This type of collaborative partnership between student teacher-cooperating teacher may lead to a positive impact on students with disabilities. To date, only one research study was conducted and did not focus only on the impact of students with disabilities and this new collaborative partnership between universities and K–12 schools.

The Center for Appropriate Dispute Resolution in Special Education (see CADRE available at: http://www.directionservice.org/cadre/) provides recommendations which apply to the idea of establishing partnerships between families, schools, and community. First, not only is it important to establish the partnerships but a mechanism needs to be in place that sustains the relationships. Second, training in collaborative skills is needed. It should not be assumed that parents or community members understand the level of collaborative skills needed or have the skills. Third, every parent's needs are different and every community has different resources. Identifying each will help establish stronger connections.

TRANSITION FROM HIGH SCHOOL TO POSTSECONDARY EDUCATION

High school serves as a springboard for postsecondary education preparation. For students with disabilities, this occurs during the transition IEP. The collaborative partnerships between family, school, and community (e.g., vocational rehabilitation) is critical. The parent-child and child-teacher partnerships formed throughout high school serves as a way to promote effective IEP planning including realistic and attainable postsecondary outcomes. In addition to the parent-child and teacher-child partnerships, additional partnerships must be established such as expanding the support system to include the guidance counselor.

POSTSECONDARY EDUCATION AND STUDENTS WITH DISABILITIES

Newman et al. (2009) report that the percentage of students with disabilities that attend a two-year postsecondary institution is similar to the general population; whereas, a significant gap exists between the percentage of students with disabilities and the general population who attend a four-year postsecondary institution.

In fact, the graduation rate is below 50 percent (Newman et al. 2009). This staggering statistic supports providing partnerships and a cascade of collaboration for students with disabilities throughout his or her lifespan.

POTENTIAL BARRIER FOR PARTNERSHIPS AT THE POSTSECONDARY LEVEL

The type of collaborative partnerships and relationships between family-school-community at the postsecondary level are the same; however, a shift of responsibility to initiate the collaborative partnerships occurs.

In K–12 education, information for the student was sent to the family; whereas, information at the postsecondary level is not sent to parents due to legislation and mandates such as the Family Educational Rights and Privacy Act (FERPA). This may be difficult for students as the parent and/or family has been the main source of emotional and academic support.

Students can waive their FERPA rights to allow parents to have access and receive specified information. Parents can continue to be a mentor and an advocate for the student but now must do so from a secondary position. In a parent brief, NCSET (2002) states that "active parent involvement fosters, not hinders, self-determination" (p. 3). So the parent should remain an active part of the collaborative team.

Information about disability services is often conveyed to students through the course syllabi. This may not be sufficient for the majority of students with disabilities. It is incumbent on the student to reach out to Disability Services. Because the level of collaborative support from disabilities services varies among institutions, students should research the types of support that is available at the institution before selecting a college or university.

The student can move the level of collaboration from informing to involving or even engaging through sustained effort and a plan of action. The plan of action begins with the student reaching out to the director of Disability Services at the institution.

At the postsecondary level, the student decides about the level of collaborative partnership with his or her parent. If the student decides to include the parent in the partnership then both student-parent can interact with disability services staff members to establish accommodations. In addition, a collaborative partnership between student-faculty must be established to ensure that accommodations are provided.

At the postsecondary level with a shift in the student taking the responsibility to establish the collaborative partnerships more peer-peer collaborative partnerships are established. For example, mentoring and peer support groups are usually available at the postsecondary level.

TRANSITION SUMMER PROGRAMS

Transition summer programs usually occur a semester before beginning freshman year. This allows students the opportunity to visit the campus before courses begin. Generally, students stay on campus for several days to a few weeks. This may be the first time the student has been away from home and had to live with another person. The student will have the opportunity to take courses or workshops on topics such as time management, test taking, and note taking.

Usually, the university provides upper-class student mentors to help the students during the week. The student will have the opportunity to explore resources within the university and the local communities. Resources within the institution may include a learning resource center, health services, tutoring center, and library services.

Having the opportunity to become familiar with the surrounding community may also be important to the student. Participating in the transition program will allow the student to develop friendships that will be important throughout the year. This will serve as the beginning of a social support system for the student with disabilities.

PEER-TO-PEER PARTNERSHIPS

Another support option that is often available for students is the peer support group. Peer support groups can be formal (developed by Disability Services) or informal (developed by students). Sometimes students with disabilities have difficulty forming positive social relationships so this will provide students with disabilities a safe environment to develop relationships.

The peer support group can explore problems and issues that students are experiencing. Upperclass students can provide leadership and act as role models for the freshmen students. Peer support groups can provide support in the areas of social, academic, and career experienced students can serve as a mentor in one to one mentoring program. The student and the mentor can be matched by disability and major area of study. The mentor can help the student learn to navigate the institution's systems.

FACULTY-STUDENT COLLABORATIVE PARTNERSHIPS

Faculty are often interested in working with students with disabilities but are unsure what to do. Faculty may receive little or no training on how to meet the needs of students with disabilities in their classroom. Faculty may feel uncomfortable speaking to students with disabilities as they are unsure of the legal responsibilities, may lack knowledge of the specific disability, and may not understand the expectation of the institution regarding students with disabilities.

Traditionally, it was the responsibility of the institution to provide training and support for faculty to learn how to effectively work with students with disabilities. This responsibility ultimately fell upon the director of Disability Services. In some cases, where there are teacher preparation programs that prepare special education teachers, these faculties are called upon to provide the training.

That said, within the proposed model of establishing partnerships with all major stakeholders, postsecondary education may want to consider having the student or family member provide the training for faculty. In return, the faculty can provide additional resources and support through community events. This model supports interaction at the family-school-community level at the postsecondary level.

The DO IT center at the University of Washington has designed training for faculty in the areas of legal issues, universal design, appropriate accommodations, and strategies. Faculty that have professional development regarding legal issues and accommodations and strategies, support from the institution, and positive personal beliefs about students with disabilities will be more effective in providing accommodations (Zhang et al. 2010).

Faculty that are comfortable speaking with students with disabilities and discussing appropriate accommodations and strategies can become a contributing member of the system of support for the student.

TEACHER PREPARATION PROGRAMS

A little explored resource at many institutions is the teacher preparation programs. The director of Disability Services and the director of Teaching Preparation programs could collaborate to design programs that meet the needs of both sets of students. There are opportunities to partner students with disabilities with teacher education candidates. Teacher candidates are being prepared to enter the K–12 classroom to meet the learning needs of all students including students with disabilities.

The teacher candidate could work in a tutoring situation with the student with disabilities. An important skill the teacher candidate must learn is how to serve as an advocate for the K–12 student population. The teacher in the K–12 system serves as the student's advocate through the RTI process. At the institution level the teacher candidate could serve as a peer advocate. The teacher candidate could assist the student through role playing and support the student in meetings with professors.

The teacher candidate brings institutional experience to the collaborative relationship as well as classroom theory. Both of these opportunities could be set up as activities/assignments within education courses or projects as part of a Future Teachers club or optional activities. The student with disabilities will be able to add a teacher candidate as part of the collaborative team while the teacher candidate will have opportunities to utilize the classroom theory in practice.

The transition from high school to postsecondary education begins with a solid support team consisting of the student, parent, special education teacher, and the guidance counselor. The team functions may begin at the informing level but through continued effort moves to the engaging level with all focused on the goal of college and career readiness.

Another underutilized resource for increasing collaboration for students with disabilities is the potential collaborative relationship between teacher preparation programs and K–12 school systems. Teacher preparation programs place students in K–12 classrooms for practical experiences such as fieldwork and final internship. Another important skill is to teach the student self-advocacy skills. Van Reusen et al. (1994) define self-advocacy as "an individual's ability to effectively communicate, convey, negotiate or assert his or her own interests, desires, needs, and rights. It involves making informed decisions and taking responsibility for those decisions" (p. 2).

The parent is usually the student's first advocate. When the child goes to school, the parent along with the special education teacher/case manager become the advocate for the child. Once the student transitions to high school the student needs to take the lead in advocacy along with the support of the parent and special education teacher/case manager.

Self-advocacy can be addressed and may include but is not limited to having the student take a course on self-determination and self-advocacy, participate in group and individual counseling, and practice examples of self-advocacy situations through role playing. The goal of the collaborative relationship at all levels is that the student would be leading the process that is characterized by systematic engagement by all the stakeholders.

LEADERSHIP DEVELOPMENT

The unique situations described above for students with disabilities afford many opportunities for students and adults to develop leadership skills. The partnerships and levels of support identified enable both systems, K–12 and IHE, to plan and implement supportive processes for students with disabilities.

Students can participate in programs as described (mentoring, peer tutoring) and develop leadership capacity through collaborative work. Faculty can further leadership skills by ensuring that all students' needs are met appropriately, identifying both class, system, and student needs, and facilitate change to meet identified challenges successfully.

KEY IDEAS IN THIS CHAPTER

- Multiple opportunities for partnership support for students with disabilities at the university and K–12 levels
- Partnerships foster collaboration that benefits systems and students
- Teacher prep programs underutilized as collaborative opportunities for students with disabilities
- Policies and laws support collaborative partnerships

SUMMARY

Students with disabilities from K–16+ require a cascade of collaboration from all major stakeholders. At the postsecondary level, to continue the cascade of collaboration between family, school, and community necessitates a shift in the student with disabilities to initiate the partnerships.

Students entering postsecondary education notice many differences between K–12 versus postsecondary education. For example, an increased level of academic requirements, less direct contact with professors, and fewer course meetings may occur. The need for collaborative relationships as a support system continues into the postsecondary environment but may actually be more difficult to find.

Too often students come to postsecondary experiences without any solid understanding of the disability, its impact, and the accommodations needed. It is essential that students in high school participate fully in their transition individual educational plan conferences in order to be prepared for postsecondary situations.

To do this, the student must understand the nature and needs of the disability and be able to articulate the accommodations/modifications needed to support the student. Part of the responsibility of the support team in Disability Services is to ensure that both the parent and the student understand the disability, the student's strengths, and the impact of the disability.

Chapter Six

Leadership, Engagement, Partnership

Fern Aefsky and Toni Zetsche

The purpose of this book is to identify how collaborative leadership can facilitate building capacity through collaborative partnerships. Many partnerships were discussed thus far, including inter- and intrauniversity departments, university and K–12 schools, and schools (K–12 and university) with families and community. How do these partnerships engage stakeholders and create leaders?

UNIVERSITY PARTNERSHIPS

As described by researchers (Officer et al. 2013; Kronick, Lester, and Luter 2013), a community project of collaboration and partnership in Indiana shared resources of 1.5 million through a grant allocation to foster support for students, families, and identified the impact of institutes of higher education (IHE) engagement with K–12 school and community that impacted faculty and programmatic improvements to teaching, learning, and training of faculty in both institutions. Teacher and administrative preparation programs at IHE lend themselves to benefitting from partnerships with K–12 schools. Practitioner practice and needs can drive the change of university programs in all teacher and administrator preparation programs. Partnerships can be created with the development of an advisory task force.

At Saint Leo University in Florida, based on collaboration with the Hillsborough County School District as a Wallace Foundation partner, an advisory task force for graduation education was developed and was instrumental in changing courses, criteria for graduation, and improving students' experiences in the school setting that assisted graduates in getting jobs. What was done and why did it matter?

Graduates of the educational leadership program, practitioners (community stakeholders) from across the state of Florida, adjuncts (many current practitioners) and faculty members worked together for a two-year period to identify successes, challenges, and wishes related to instructional leadership and administrative leadership programs of study, including master's programs in reading, special education, leadership, and a postgraduate program, an educational specialist degree.

Practitioners on the task force helped to identify what skills they desired in their beginning teachers and administrators. This information was broken into strands, and then faculty matched skills to the most recent teacher leadership, InTasc and Professional (formerly ISLLC) national standards. Courses of study were realigned, and courses revised or created by faculty members to better meet the needs of students and those practitioners hiring students after graduation. The task force met a total of six times in two years. Twenty-eight new courses were developed and another twenty-seven were revised.

This collaborative work resulted in an improved program of studies for students that was aligned with "state of the art" national standards. The partnership resulted in practitioners being able to see the tangible work of their efforts, and as a result, every person continued as a task force member the following year. Trust in purpose was evident.

New programs of study were investigated and developed for potential growth of the university's programs. Support from partners provided needed data for this expansion process and created interest in those programs of studies in multiple geographical areas across the country.

University faculty are required to conduct research, do presentations at conferences, and publish their work. As a result of this advisory council work, all of those events occurred.

The K–12 practitioners who participated on the advisory task force benefited as they collaborated on research done for this purpose, were informed of state legislative and department of education initiatives, and were able to bring that information back to their districts. This enabled them to address these issues at a local level and initiated processes of change and support for their faculty and administrators. The result was shared research and conference presentations, university personnel providing professional development workshops and training that was mutually beneficial to both the university and school districts.

Leadership skills were developed and strengthened. Administrators shared information in their districts and were leaders of content knowledge, impacting positive change. Alumni used information to complete aspiring leadership applications to enter district administrative pools.

One example of a result of the collaborative work from advisory task force members is a university and K–12 partnership that led to a high school teaching academy in a local district. The collaborative partnership helped develop and support a local teacher preparation program.

River Ridge High School in Pasco County, Florida, opened a teaching academy that will prepare secondary students interested in a career in education when they enter a teacher preparation program at the university level. This teaching academy offers a sequence of courses that provide rigorous content aligned with challenging academic standards and knowledge needed to prepare for careers in the education and training career cluster. Project based learning and hands-on experiences in the field of education provide students with real world experiences in the education profession.

Students will benefit from field experiences in kindergarten through grade 12 settings as well as collaborative relationships with university students, graduates, and faculty. The collaborative partnership between River Ridge High School and Saint Leo University provides opportunities for continued growth based on the reciprocal needs between the school district and university.

Students in the program are leaders in their high school. They have a voice as they learn skills as future teachers, and were highlighted in numerous ways on local news media. These students are leaders in their quest to become teachers, and will carry these leadership skills to their postsecondary experiences.

Evidence of additional partnerships are a middle school literacy research project; a high school literacy project; a service-based project for university students and high school students through clubs; and multiple projects in elementary education classrooms for literacy projects, educational technology for improving capacity of teachers, and facilitation of instructional opportunities for students at both the university and K–12 levels. Teacher, administrative, and student leaders will emerge from this collaborative work.

Leaders and leadership capacity can be facilitated through mentorships. These relationships are important to organizational goals being met by participants in business and education. Skills and knowledge specific to the organization are learned by mentees while working with colleagues supporting leadership development for that organization.

Mentoring students and faculty members, providing professional development opportunities, sharing resources, co-presenting at conferences all are evidence of successful partnership programs. Leaders emerge from each as facilitation of partnerships grow.

A collaborative mentoring program for professional development at historically black colleges and universities (HBCUs) was established using the Collaborative Responsive Education Mentoring Model (Bryant-Shanklin and Brumage 2011). They defined mentoring as a "process involving two or more individuals working together to develop the careers and abilities of all participants" (Bryant-Shanklin and Brumage 2011, p. 43).

One of the characteristics specific to IHE of HBCU's is the relationship between university faculty and practitioners in K–12 schools. The diversity of students in schools and focus on low performing schools in high poverty areas, presents an area where collaborative research and partnerships can assist students in reaching goals successfully.

The impact of partnerships on teachers and learning has been researched by many (Curwood et al. 2011; Devin 2013; Martin 2015; Peel, Peel, and Baker 2002; Stevenson and Shetley 2015; Vernon-Dotson and Floyd 2012). Typically, research is connected to teacher and educator leadership preparatory programs.

Student leaders emerge when working on collaborative projects. Teacher leaders emerge when given opportunities to demonstrate their knowledge and expertise. Technology programs that support teacher training and equipment are frequently utilized between schools and university programs in education.

Student leaders have also emerged through partnerships between school and IHE for students with disabilities. Teachers and student retention and increased student achievement have been accomplished through effective partnerships (NYSED, Special education and Vocational and Rehabilitation Services, 2015).

Critical input and integration of resources will allow us to better understand the needs of practitioners and further develop partnerships while facilitating a discussion surrounding the benefits of collaborative partnerships with the school and classroom based educators.

The public school provides the perfect setting for putting theory into practice for university professors. University level researchers can create powerful partnerships that engage current practitioners and improve the quality of beginning teachers (including former university graduates). This type of collaborative partnership may increase student retention in both high schools and university settings.

Working collaboratively on grant sources enables both universities and K–12 partners to support collaborative efforts. Leaders from both institutions emerge, as resources are gained. Technology, STEM, special education, and leadership development for instructional leaders (both teachers and administrators) are popular for programs of education, business, and human services programs of study. In business and criminal justice programs, partnerships with appropriate agencies and corporations around issues of safety, cyber security, social justice, and internships create opportunities for successful partnerships. In all areas, students, faculty, and institutions benefit from shared resources.

Partnerships between universities and communities encourage leaders from various organizations and institutions to learn from and develop successful collaboration projects to facilitate change in their local communities

(Hopson, Miller, and Lovelace 2016). Their research supports police agencies in sustaining leadership change in difficult situations as well as helping community leaders (politicians, religious leaders) engage community members in leadership activities.

A significant challenge is sustaining partnerships across IHE departments and schools, departments of education for teacher and educational administration preparatory programs, and between universities, K–12 schools, and community businesses and agencies. All stakeholders can be positively engaged and share in benefits from collaborative partnerships. Sustainable leaders and succession for leaders result from these partnerships, inclusive of students, faculty members, managers, and leaders in organizations (businesses, agencies).

K–12 PARTNERSHIPS

Schools in K–12 systems have established partnerships historically focused on student activities (sports, clubs, tutoring/mentoring), parents (PTA/PTOs), and state requirements (advisory committees, shared decision making). However, a renewed focus on partnerships has risen due to new federal regulations and focus.

Research in each discipline identifies strengths and challenges. Connecting those areas through partnerships builds leaders of all constituencies that strengthen organizational goals.

In the global business world, many authors have focused on collaboration and leadership (Barsh and Lavoie 2014; Gardner 2009; Goleman and Boyatzis 2013; Hewertson 2015; Maxwell 2013). Literature supports multiple types of leadership style theories and they are applicable in both educational and organizational leadership entities.

The military has multiple leadership programs in each branch, and for different purposes. Leadership by Example is one program that supports leaders in the military and transition to employment post-military career for veterans (Storlie 2015). Leveled leadership, the impact leaders have on decision making, critical analysis, and other components are equal to those in business and education-communication, collaboration, goals, mission, accountability, and organizational change.

MOTIVATIONAL QUALITIES

Leaders are given the task of creating motivational support through a variety of challenging issues through all organizations. There will be times when motivating others is required, even when the topic is not motivating the leader on a personal level. It takes courage to be a leader and what leaders do with that intent results in success or lack of success as a leader. Gordon (2014) described a story where courage was described: "No challenge can stop you if you have the courage to keep moving forward in the face of your greatest fears and biggest challenges. Be courageous!"

CHANGE PROCESS

Thinking about our cultural beliefs and biases as leaders is important, as the individual leaders deal with come from a broad group of people of various backgrounds. It is difficult to park our own value systems as we try to better understand our stakeholders and their backgrounds and beliefs. However, good leaders need to acknowledge their own beliefs and biases in order to view others and be able to think about common attributes and goals.

Working with many people of varied backgrounds, a true understanding of value systems and how they impact others is warranted. In order to build relationships with others from different backgrounds, these concepts must be considered, understood, and used to foster positive relationship and partnerships.

The concepts of trust and relationships are important. Maxwell (2013) discusses how good leadership changes individual lives, builds organizations, and impacts communities. Educators are held accountable for student achievement. Other organizational leaders are accountable for their organizational success (profit, meeting growth goals, etc.).

Engaging others through leadership and stakeholder partnerships is a critical measure of accountability. Leaders need to recognize and facilitate the process of this work, creating a cycle of identification, measuring feedback, and instituting needed change. Strategic development of this process and communication of this process are steps that need to be developed and executed in order for a cycle of accountability to be achieved.

Persistence matters. There will be challenges along the way to meeting goals and creating a framework with stakeholders for achieving those goals. Leaders' expectations of those challenges will enable proactive thoughts and planning toward goal acquisition.

Literature supports multiple types of leadership, including distributive, hierarchal, transformational, transactional, and autocratic or bureaucratic leadership. Leadership is often defined as a process of influencing how others think or act and the consequences of those results. One mistake many leaders make is the assumption that only their actions result in leadership attributes. However, the reactions of others create a domino effect of additional emergent leaders in the organization.

A balance needs to be established between words and actions. A good leader communicates expectations, solicits information from various sources and its stakeholders, and delegates tasks. Gathering all the information from others that results in leadership decisions is the responsibility of the leader.

People are typically resistant to change. There has been a lot of discussion and research about the importance of organizational culture and climate. Identification of organizational components must be specified prior to making change.

Change is difficult in any organization. In spite of the reason for change, there will always be a minimum of three group reactions to change:

- The group who wants everything to stay the way it is and sees no value in change.
- Those who see change as an opportunity because they did not like the status quo.
- The group who doesn't care either way.

A successful leader needs to understand the dynamics of each group and recognize diversity issues of each group and their impact on stakeholders.

KEY IDEAS OF THIS CHAPTER

- Change process
- Similarities across disciplines in developing leaders
- Diversity considerations
- Examples of collaborative partnerships
- Leadership development through partnership activities

SUMMARY

Meaningful relationships, shared visions and focus, resiliency, and support are supported by collaborative partnerships. The sustainability of leaders at all levels of university and K–12 systems requires a concentrated effort on building leadership capacity through partnerships.

Leaders who leave an impact on systems by creating a framework for leadership of stakeholders will enable schools and universities to continue to grow, meet the needs of students, faculty, staff, and community, and provide resources beneficial to all stakeholders.

Bibliography

A Blueprint for Reform of the Reauthorization of the Elementary and Secondary Education Act, United States Department of Education, March 2010.

Adams, W. 2015. Extending the Common Ground. Yale–New Haven Teachers Institute, #15, Fall 2015, p. 4.

Aefsky, F. 2016. Two Chapters: Educational Leadership; Differentiated Instruction; The Apple Shouldn't Fall far from the Common Core. Rowman & Littlefield.

Allen, J. 2007. Creating welcoming schools. Teachers College Press, Columbia University.

Amendt, T. 2008. Involvement to engagement: community education practices in a suburban and an inner-city community school. *Unpublished Master's thesis.* University of Saskatchewan, Saskatoon, Canada.

Ammentorp, L. and L. Madden. 2104. Partnered Placements: Creating and Supporting Successful Collaboration among Preservice Teachers. *Journal of Early Childhood Teacher Education*, 35:135 –49.

Amrein-Beardsley, A., J. Barnett, T. Ganesh, G. Tirupalavanum. 2013. Seven Legitimate Apprehensions about Evaluating Teacher Education Programs. *Teachers College Record* 115:12.

Angeli, C. and N. Valanides. 2009. Instructional effects on critical thinking: Performance on ill-defined issues, European Association for Research on Learning and Instruction.

Auerbach, S. 2011. From moral supporters to struggling advocates: Reconceptualizing parent roles in education through the experiences of working-class families of color. *Urban Education, 42*(3), 250–83.

Auerbach, S. 2007. From moral supporters to struggling advocates. *Urban Education, 42*(3), 250 –83.

Baker, V. L., Pifer, M. J., & Flemion, B. (2013). "Process challenges and learning-based interactions in stage 2 of doctoral education: Implications from two applied social science fields." *Journal of Higher Education, 84*(4), 449-476.

Baker, V. and M. Pifer. 2011. The role of relationships in the transition from doctoral student to independent scholar. *Studies in Continuing Education*, 33:1, 5–17.

Barnyak, N. and T. McNelly. 2009. *The School Community Journal*, 19(1):33 –58.

Barsh, J. and J. Lavoie. 2104. Centered Leadership. Crown Publishing, NY.

Bastian, J. J. (2010) *Exploring parental perception of involvement with college students.* Available from ERIC. (860368186; ED516520). Retrieved from http://search.proquest.com.ezproxylocal.library.nova.edu/docview/860368186?accountid=6579M

Bensley, D. 2010. Teaching and Assessing Critical Thinking Skills for Argument Analysis in Psychology. *Teaching of Psychology* 37(2):91 –96

Benson, F. and S. Martin. 2003. Organizing successful parent involvement in urban schools. *Child Study Journal*, 33(3):187–93.

Beshears, J. and F. Gino. 2015. Leaders as decision architects. Harvard Business Review.

Blasé, J. and J. Blasé. 2000. "Effective instructional leadership: Teachers' perspectives on how principals promote teaching and learning in schools." *Journal of Educational Administration*, Vol. 38 Iss: 2, pp. 130–41.

Bohm, D. 1965. The special theory of relativity. WA Benjamin: NY.

Boylan, M. (2016). "Deepening system leadership: Teachers leading from below." *Educational Management Administration & Leadership, 44*(1), 57-72. Retrieved from http://search.proquest.com.ezproxylocal.library.nova.edu/docview/1773226809?accountid=6579

Breci, M. G. 1994. Higher education for law enforcement: The Minnesota model. *FBI Law Enforcement Bulletin,* 63(1):1–4.

Brookfield, S. D. 2011. Teaching for critical thinking: Tools and techniques to help students question their assumptions. San Francisco, CA: Jossey-Bass.

Brown, E. and S. Kinsella. 2006. University/community partnerships: Engaging human service and social work students in service learning. *Human Service Education*, 26(1):59–73.

Bryant-Shanklin, M. and N. Brumage. 2011. Collaborative responsive education mentoring. *Florida Journal of Educational Administration and Policy*. Fall 2011 5(1).

Bryk, A. S., L. M. Gomez, and A. Grunow. 2010. Getting ideas into action: Building networked improvement communities in education. Stanford, CA: Carnegie Foundation for the Advancement of Teaching.

Bryk, A. S., L. M. Gomez, A. Grunow, and P. G. LeMahieu. 2015. Learning to improve: How America's schools can get better.

Burdman, P. 2008. Does California Master Plan Still Work? *Harvard Business Review*, July 2008, 135–40.

Burrows, J. 1999. Going beyond labels: A framework for profiling institutional stakeholders.

Calvert, V. 2011. Service learning to social entrepreneurship: A continuum of action learning. *Journal of Higher Education Theory and Practice*, 11(2):118–29.

Campbell, E. and C. Lassiter. 2010. From Collaborative Ethnography to Collaborative Pedagogy. *Anthropology and Education Quarterly*, 41(4):370–85.

Canfield, J. 2015. The Success Principles. Harper Collins: NY.

Carlan, P. and F. Byxbe. 2000. The promise of humanistic policing: Is higher education living up to societal expectation. *American Journal of Criminal Justice,* 24, 2.

Caruso, N. 2000. Lessons learned in a city-school social services partnership. *Social Work in Education*, 22(2):108–16.

Celano, C. and S. Neuman. 2016. Libraries at the Ready. *Educational leadership*, 73(5):74–77.

Chappell, A. T. 2009. The philosophical versus actual adoption of community policing: A case study. *Criminal Justice Review, 34*(1):5–28.

Chrisman, V. 2005. How Schools Sustain Success. Educational Leadership, February 2005, 16–20.

Chrispeels, J. H., P. H. Burke, P. Johnson, and A. J. Daly. 2008. Aligning mental models of district and school leadership teams for reform coherence. *Education and Urban Society*, 40(730):1–22. doi: 10.1177/0013124508319582.

Christianden, et al. 2011. Disrupting college. Washington, D.C. Center for American Progress.

Clark, R. 2007. Journalism and education for the public good. *Catalyst for Change*, 35(1):9–21.

Cohen, D. 2005. The heart of change field guide. MA: Harvard Business School Press.

Colombo, M. May 2004. Family Literacy Nights. *Educational Leadership*, 61(8):48–51.

Connell, N. M., K. Miggans, and J. M. McGloin. 2008. Can a community policing initiative reduce serious crime? A local evaluation. *Police Quarterly* 11(2):127–50.

Cook, L. and M. Friend. 1995. Co-Teaching: Guidelines for creating effective practices.

Cruz, G. Parent Academies: How schools are helping moms and dads do more for their kids. *Time*. November 16, 2009.

Curwood, et. al (2011). "Building Effective Community-University Partnerships: Are Universities Truly Ready?" *Michigan Journal of Community Service Learning*. 15-26.

Dalgleish, D. and A. Myhill. 2004. "Reassuring the Public: A Review of International Policing Interventions." London: Home Office www.homeoffice.gov.uk/rds/pdfs04/r241.pdf.

Daniel, G. 2011. Family-school partnerships: towards sustainable pedagogical practice. *Asia-Pacific Journal of Teacher Education, 39*(2):165–76.

Danielson, C. 2009. Teacher Leadership that Strengthens Professional Practice. ASCD, VA.

Darch, C., Miao, Y., & Shippen, P. (2004). "A model for involving parents of children with learning and behavior problems in the schools." *Preventing School Failure, 48*(3), 24-34.

Datnow, A., and S. Stringfield. (2000). *Working together for reliable school reform.* Retrieved from: Deal, T., and K. Peterson. 1999. Shaping school culture: The heart of leadership. http://search.proquest.com.ezproxylocal.library.nova.edu/docview/62451951?accountid=6579

Delattre, E. 2006. *Character and Cops: Ethics in Policing, Fifth Edition.* Washington, DC: American Enterprise Institute Press, www.aei.org/docLib/9780844742175.pdf.

Delmont, T. 2011. Resolving Issues in Innovative Graduate Degree Programs: The Metropolitan State University Doctor of Business Administration Experience. *American Journal of Business Education*, vol. 4, n. 3, 63–68.

Dentzau, M. 2014. The Value of Place. *Cultural studies of science education.* 9(1):165–71. Department of Justice, Bureau of Justice Statistics.

Devin, M. 2013. Case Study in the Power of Collaboration. *Educational Consideration*, vol. 41, n. 6 –11.

Diamond, D. and M. Weiss. 2009. Community Policing Looking Towards Tomorrow, http://ric-zai-inc.com/ric.php?page=detail&id=COPS-W0520.

Didier, J. M. *Evaluating cadet leadership positions at the U.S. air force academy.* Available from ERIC. (1651839980; ED550353). Retrieved from http://search.proquest.com.ezproxylocal.library.nova.edu/docview/1651839980?accountid=6579

District School Board of Pasco County (DSBPC), 2003. BEST Program Proposal, 1–20.

Districts promote family engagement, Harvard Family Research Project, Issue brief, 1–16.

Division of Vocational Rehabilitation (n.d.). Retrieved September 3, 2015 from: http://www.rehabworks.org/ doi:http://dx.doi.org/10.1007/s10551-008-9677-4.

Donald, R. 2012. Tapia School of Business Five-Year Strategic Plan.

DuFour, R. May 2004. Schools as Learning Communities. *Educational Leadership*, 61(8):6 –11.

DuFour, R., and M. Mattos. 2013. How do principals really improve schools? *Educational Leadership,* 70(7):34–40.

DuFour, R., and M. Fullan. 2013. Cultures built to last: Making PLC's systemic. Bloomington, IN: Solution Tree.

Dunne, B. 2016. Building bonds between teachers and their cities: Boston's historical partnership PD series. Retrieved 8/15/2016 from: http://inservice.ascd.org/building-bonds-between-teachers-and-their-cities-bostons-historical-partnership-pd-series/.

Dweck, C. 2006. Mindset: The New Psychology of Success. Ballantine: NY.

Eaker, R., DuFour, R., & Burnette, R. (2002). *Getting started: Reculturing schools to become professional learning communities.* Bloomington, IN: National Educational Service. Retrieved from http://search.proquest.com.ezproxylocal.library.nova.edu/docview/62198947?accountid=6579

Eberly, J., A. Joshi, and J. Konzal. 2007. *The School Community Journal,* 17(2):7 –26. Communicating with Families Across Cultures: An investigation of teacher perceptions and practices. Educational Foundation. *Educational Leadership,* 61(7):48–51.

Emfinger, K. 2012. Literacy readiness: transitional partnerships between pre-school and kindergarten. *Childhood education,* 88(4):258–65.

Epstein, J. 2001. School, family and community partnerships. Westview: CO.

Erlandson, D. 1993. Doing naturalistic inquiry. A guide to methods. SAGE: CA.

European Commission. 2014. Europe 2020 in a nutshell. Retrieved from: http://ec.europa.eu/europe2020/europe-2020-in-a-nutshell/index_en.htm.

European Commission. August 17, 2011. Europe 2020 Targets. Retrieved from: http://ec.europa.eu/europe2020/targets/eu-targets/index_en.htm.

European Commission. March 19, 2014. Taking stock of the Europe 2020 strategy for smart sustainable and inclusive growth. Communication from the commission to the European

Parliament, the Council, the European Economic and Social Committee and the Committee of the Regions. Retrieved from: http://ec.europa.eu/europe2020/pdf/europe2020stocktaking_en.pdf.

Every Student Succeed Act (ESSA). 2016. 114th Congress (2015–2016). HR.5-Student Success Act.

Fassin, Y. 2009. The stakeholder model refined. *Journal of Business Ethics,* 84(1):113–35.

Feldman, J., K. Feighan, E. Kirtcheva, and E. Heeren. 2012. Aiming High: Exploring the Influence of Implementarion Fidelity and Cognitive Demand Levels on Struggling Readers' Literacy Outcomes. *Journal of Classroom Interaction,* 47(1):4 –10.

Fennel, M. 2016. What educators need to know about ESSA. *Educational Leadership,* Summer 2016, 62 –65.

Fisher, R. 1994. Let the people decide. Twayne: NY.

Florida Department of Law Enforcement. 2014. Florida Law Enforcement Academy, Vol. 1, ISBN 13: 978-1-58390-128-1 ISBN 10: 1-58390-128-1.

Forbes, K. J. (2001). "Students and their parents. Where do campuses fit in?" *About Campus,* 6(4), 11-17.

Freeman, R. E. 1983. Stockholders and stakeholders: A new perspective on corporate governance. *California Management Review (Pre-1986),* 25(000003), 88. Retrieved from: http://search.proquest.com.ezproxy.saintleo.edu/docview/206241787?accountid=4870.

Freeman, R. E. 2004. The stakeholder approach revisited. *Zeitschrift Für Wirtschafts-Und Unternehmensethik,* 5(3):228–41. Retrieved from http://search.proquest.com.ezproxy.saintleo.edu/docview/225264646?accountid=4870.

Freire, P. (1998). "Cultural action and conscientization." *Harvard Educational Review,* 68(4), 499-521.

Fry, P. 2015. Extending the Common Ground. Yale-New Haven Teachers Institute, #15, Fall 2015, p. 2.

Fullan, M., P. Hill, and C. Crevola. 2006. Breakthrough. CA: Corwin Press.

Gardner, D. 2011. Characteristic Collaborative Processes in School-University Partnerships. *Planning and Changing,* vol. 42, no. ½, 63 –69.

Gardner, H. 2009. Breaking down barriers to Collaboration. Retrieved from: HBR.org.

Gillis, J. 2011. Global leadership development. (Doctoral dissertation.) Retrieved from ProQuest Dissertations and Theses database. UMI No. 3455394.

Godinez, E., and Leslie, B. B. (2015). "Army civilian leadership development: Self-efficacy, choice, and learning transfer." *Adult Learning,* 26(3), 93-100.

Goleman, D. 2000. Leadership That Gets Results. *Harvard Business Review,* 78(2), 78–90.

Goleman, D., and R. Boyatzis. 2013. The focused leader. *Harvard Business Review,* 91, 51–60. Retrieved from: http://search.proquest.com.ezproxylocal.library.nova.edu/docview/1465267520?accountid=6579.

Goodman, N. 2012. The crisis in the global leadership pipeline. *Training.* May/June 2012, 66–67.

Goorian, B. 2000. Alternative teacher compensation. ERIC Digest 142, Clearinghouse on Educational Management, University of Oregon.

Grim, S. D.; Medina, M. A.; Bringle, R. G.; & Foreman, A. (2013). "Strengthening community schools through university partnerships." *Peabody Journal of Education,* 88(5), 564-577.

Haines, et al. 2015. Research and Practice for Persons with Severe Disabilities. 40(3):227–39.

Hall, Peter. 2008. Building Bridges: Strengthening the Principal Induction Process Through Intentional Mentoring. Phi Delta Kappan, February 2008.

Hallinger, P., and R. Heck. 1996. Reassessing the principal's role in school effectiveness: A review of empirical research, 1980–1995. *Educational Administration Quarterly,* 32(1)5–44.

Harris, L.; Salzman; Frantz; Newsome; and Martin. 2016. Using Accountability Measures in the Preparation of Preservice Teachers. Paper.

Harvard Family Research Project. April 2010. Family Engagement as a Systemic, sustained and Integrated Strategy to Promote Student Achievement.

Hattie, J. 2009. *Visible Learning: A synthesis of over 800 meta-analyses related to achievement.* Abingdon, Oxon: Routledge.

HBR's 10 must reads. On Collaboration. Harvard Business School Publishing.

Hedeen, T., P. Moses, and M. Peter. (n.d). Encouraging meaningful parent/educator collabora-tion: A review of recent literature. Center for Appropriate Dispute Resolution in Special Education: Eugene, OR. Retrieved from: http://pacfamilyresourcecenter.pbworks.com/w/file/fetch/49649955/CADRE_Meaningful%20Collaboration.pdf.

Heifetz, R. 1994. Leadership without easy answers. Cambridge, MA: Belknap Press.

Henderson, A. T., K. L. Mapp, V. R. Johnson, and D. Davies. 2007. Beyond the bake sale: The essential guide to family-school partnerships. New York: The New Press, Retrieved from: http://search.proquest.com.ezproxylocal.library.nova.edu/docview/912451942?accountid=6579.

Herman, et. al. 2016. School Leadership Interventions under ESSA. Rand Corporation, vol. 1.

Hess, K., and C. Orthmann. 2012. *Management and supervision in law enforcement* (6th ed.). New York: Delmar Cengage Learning.

Hewertson, R. B. 2015. Lead like it matters . . . because it does: Practical leadership tools to inspire and engage your people and create great results. McGraw Hill Education.

Hickman, M., and B. Reaves. 2006. *Local police departments*. Washington, DC.

Hindin, A. (2010). "Linking home and school: Teacher candidates' beliefs and experiences." *School Community Journal, 20*(2), 73-90.

Holloway, John H. Research Link: Mentoring New Leaders. *Educational Leadership*, April 2004.

Hopson, R., P. Miller, and T. Lovelace. 2016. University-School-community Partnerships as Vehicle for Leadership, Service and Change. Leadership and Policy in Schools 15 (1), 26–44.

Hudson, D. December 1, 2014. *Building Trust Between Communities and Local Police*.

Hull, J. 2012. Center for Public Education. Retrieved from: http://www.centerforpubliceducation.org/principal-perspective.

Hulpia, H., Devos, G., and Van Kerr, H (2011). "The relation between school leadership from a distributed perspective and teachers' organizational commitment." *Educational Administra-tion quarterly, 47*(5): 728-771.

Ignatius, A. 2015. Becoming a leader, becoming yourself. *Harvard Business Review*, 93(5), 10.

Ishimaru, A. (2014). "Rewriting the rules of engagement: Elaborating a model of district-community collaboration." *Harvard Educational Review, 84*(2). 188-203.

Jenkins, B. 2008. What it takes to be an instructional leader. National Association of Elemen-tary School Principals. Alexandria, VA: NAESP.

Johnston, W., J. Kaufman, and L. Thompson. 2106. Rand Corporation Report.

Jones, S., G. Lefore, M. Harvey, and K. Ryland. 2012. Distributed leadership: a collaborative framework for academics, executives and professionals in higher education. *Journal of Higher Education Policy and Management*, vol. 34, no.1, February 2012, 67–78.

Jongbloed, B., J. Enders, and C. Salerno. 2008. Higher education and its communities. *Journal of Community Service Learning*, Spring 2011, 15 –20.

Kappeler, V. E., and L. K. Gaines. 2005. *Community policing: contemporary perspective* (4th ed.). Cincinnati, OH: Anderson Publishing.

Kepic, G. (2006). "Causes and implications of parental involvement in the advising process." Retrieved April 19, 2008, from NACADA Clearinghouse of Academic Advising Resources web site at http://www.nacada.KSU.edu/.../AdvisingIssues/Parental-Involvement.html

Kincaid, S. 2009. Defining human services: A discourse analysis. *Human Service Education*, 29(1)14–24

Kirschner, P. A., J. Sweller, and R. E. Clark 2006. *Educational Psychologist*, 41(2):75–86. Lawrence Erlbaum Associates, Inc.

Knowles, M. S., R. A. Swanson, and E. F. Holton III. 2005. *The adult learner: The definitive classic in adult education and human resource development* (8th ed.). New York: Rout-ledge.

Kouzes, J. & B. Posner. 2010. The truth about Leadership. Jossey-Bass: CA.

Kronick, R. F., J. N. Lester, D. G. Luter. *Peabody Journal of Education*, 88.5 (November 2013): 657 –64

Kruger, M., B. Witziers, and P. Sleegers. 2007. The impact of school leadership on school level factors: Validation of causal model. School Effectiveness and School Improvement, 18(1), 1-20. doi: 10.1080/09243450600797638.

Kyvik, S., & T. B. Olsen. 2012. The relevance of doctoral training in different labour markets. *Journal of Education and Work*, 25(2):205–24.

Lambert, L. 2003. *Leadership capacity for lasting school improvement.* Association for Supervision and Curriculum Development (ASCD). Alexandria, VA.

Lambert, L. 2006. Lasting leadership: A study of high leadership capacity schools. The *Educational Forum,* 70(3):238–54.

Lange, D. K., and Stone, M. E. (2001). *Parental involvement in admissions and financial aid* Retrieved   from   http://search.proquest.com.ezproxylocal.library.nova.edu/docview/62261004?accountid=6579

Lashway, L. 2003. Transforming principal preparation. *ERIC Digest, 165.* Retrieved from:http://eric.uoregon.edu/publications/digests/digestl65.html.

Layton, L. 2014. Education department moves to regulate teacher preparation programs.

Litz, D. 2011. Globalization and the changing face of educational leadership: Current trends and emerging dilemmas. *International Education Studies,* 4(3), 47–61.

Lopez, S., A. Torres, and P. Norwood. 1998. Building partnerships: A successful collaborative experience between social work and education. *Social Work in Education,* 20(3):165–76.

Lutz, F. W. and C. Merz. 1992. *Journal of School Leadership*, 2 (3, 4).

Lynch, R. (2006). "Arts and community colleges: Vital partnerships for creative communities." *Community College Journal, 76*(3), 42-45.

MacTavish, K., M. McClelland, L. Gray, S. Bowman, P. Moran, L. Burgy. 2006.

Madden, D., D. Lynch, and T. Doe. 2015. Teacher researchers: Creating the outstanding school. London: UK.

Mapp, K. 2008. Making the Connection Between Families and Schools. Harvard University presentation.

Mapp, K. and P. Kuttner. 2013. Partners in education: A dual capacity building framework for family-school partners. Austin, TX: SEDL.

Marcus, J. 2008. The Engaged University. *Harvard Business Review*, Fall 2008, 125–28.

Marshall, M. and P. Shah, P. 2014. Linking the process and outcome of parent involvement policy to the parent involvement gap.

Martin, D. 2015. Complex School-University Partnerships. Doctoral dissertation. Retrieved from: ProQuest #3731020.

Marzano, R. and T. Waters. 2013. School Leadership that Works. ASCD, Alexandria: VA.

Marzano, R. J., T. Waters, and B. A. McNulty. 2005. *School leadership that works: From research to results.* Alexandria, VA: ASCD.

Maxwell, J. 2010. Everyone Communicates, Few Connect. Nashville, TN. Thomas Nelson.

Maxwell, J. 2013. How Successful People Lead. Center Street: NY. May 2015, 5262.

McLeskey, J., & N. L. Waldron. 2015. Effective leadership makes schools truly inclusive. *Phi Delta Kappan*, 96(5):68–73.

Mileski, K., A. Mohamed, and R. Hunter. 2014. Creating inclusive spaces for partnerships. *Gateways: International Journal of Community Research and Engagement*, vol. 7:144–56.

Mitchell, R. M., L. A. W. Kensler, and M. Tschannen-Moran, M. January 1, 2015. Examining the Effects of Instructional Leadership on School Academic Press and Student Achievement. *Journal of School Leadership, 25, 2,* 223–51.

Mooney, J. and R. Tourse. 1999. *Collaborative practice: School and human service partnerships.* Westport, CT: Praeger Publishers.

Morabito, M. S. 2010. Understanding community policing as an innovation: Patterns of adoption. *Crime & Delinquency,* 56(4), 564–87.

Murphy, K. 2013. Parent involvement and student retention. Washington State University.

National Association of Elementary School Principals. 2001. Leading learning communities: Standards for what principals should know and be able to do. Alexandria, VA: Author.

National Policy Board for Educational Administration. 2015. Professional Standards for Educational Leaders. Reston: VA.

National PTA. 1997. National standards for parent/family involvement programs. Report UD.

Naugle, K., and T. A. Campbell. (n.d.). Post-secondary transition model for students with disabilities. Retrieved September 10, 2015 from: http://JSC.Montana.edu/articles/v8n40.

Nelson, S. W., and Guerra, P. L. (2014). "Educator beliefs and cultural knowledge: Implications for school improvement efforts." *Educational Administration Quarterly, 50*(1), 67-95.

Ness, M. et al. (2010). The Growth of Higher Educators for Social Justice: Collaborative.

Newman, L., M. Wagner, R. Cameto, and A. M. Knokey. 2009. The post-high school outcomes of youth with disabilities up to 4 years after high school: A report from the national longitudinal transition study-2 (NLTS2). *National Center for Special Education Research 2009–3017*, ED 505448.

Nolan, J, et. al. (2009). "The Penn State College Elementary Professional School Collaborative." *School-University Partnerships, 3*(2). 19-30.

Noland, B. 2011. The West Virginia Experience. *Harvard Business Review*, May, 2011, 305 –307.

Obrien, A. 2014. When Teachers and Administrators Collaborate. Edutopia, Georgia Lucas.

Odden, A. 2011. Schools can still improve. *Educational Leadership*, 69(4):14.

Orphanos, S. and M. Orr. 2014. Learning leadership matters. *Educational Management Administration and Leadership*, 42(5):680–700.

Ouellette, P., R. Briscoe, and C. Tyson. 2004. Parent-school and community partnerships in children's mental health: Networking challenges, dilemmas, and solutions. *Journal of Child and Family Studies,* 13(3):295–308.

Owens, R., and T. Valesky. 2007. Organizational behavior in education: Adaptive Leadership and School Reform. Boston, MA: Pearson Education Inc.

Pace, J. 2000. Pedagogical Methodologies in Teaching Critical Thinking Skills to Basic Police Recruits at Madison Area Technical College.

Parent Brief: Promoting effective parent involvement in secondary education transition. 2002. NCSET. Retrieved September 4, 2015 from: http://www.ncset.org/publications/viewdesc. asp?id=208.

Parent Involvement Center 2012. Retrieved from: http://www.parentinvolvement.ca/principals. htm.

Paul, R. and L. Elder. 2010. *The Miniature Guide to Critical Thinking Concepts and Tools.* Dillon Beach, CA: Foundation for Critical Thinking Press.

Payne, B. and D. Button. 2009. Legislative Patterns and Implications for Community Corrections Officers. *Criminal Justice Policy Review* December 2009, vol. 20, no. 4, 414 –36.

Peel, H., B. Peel, and M. Baker. 2002. School/university partnerships: a viable model.

Peters, April. 2010. Elements of a Successful Mentoring of a Female School Leader. *Leadership and Policy Studies in Schools*, Vol. 9, pp. 108–29.

Petersen, J. and D. Treagust. 2014. School and University Partnerships. *Australian Journal of Teacher Education*, 39(9).

Peterson, K. "The professional development of principle innovations." *Opportunities, Educational Administration Quarterly*, vol 38, No.2, 2002.

Pisano, G. and R. Verganti. 2013. Which Kind of Collaboration Is Right for You? Chapter HBR's 10 must reads. On Collaboration, Harvard Business School Publishing.

Place-based Education Evaluation Collaborative. 2010. *The Benefits of Place-based Education: A Report from the Place-based Education Evaluation Collaborative.* Retrieved 8/21/2016 from: http://tinyurl.com/PEECBrochure.

Price, H. 2008. Transformational leadership. In A. Martuno & Gosling (eds.). Leadership. The key concepts. London: Routledge.

Priestly, A. et al. 2015. Pathways to success: AIME's educational mentoring model. *Learning communities: international journal of learning in social contexts,* 17, 44–53.

Professional Development in Higher Education. Insight: A Journal of Scholarly Professional Learning Communities. Bloomington, IN: National Educational Service.

Protecting Civil Rights: A Leadership Guide for State, Local and Tribal Law Enforcement. Alexandria, Virginia: International Association of Chiefs of Police, September 2006. Retrieved from: www.cops.usdoj.gov/files/ric/Publications/e06064100.pdf.

Protsik, J. 1996. *History of teacher pay and incentive reforms.* Retrieved from: http://search. proquest.com.ezproxylocal.library.nova.edu/docview/62695581?accountid=6579.

Purdy, J., and J. Lawless, J. February 2012. Learning about governance through nonprofit board service. *Journal of Management Education*, 36(1):33–65.

Ravitch, D. 2010. The Death and Life of the Great American School System: how testing and choice are undermining education. Basic Books, Philadelphia, PA.

Reeves, Doug, 2009. *Leading change in your school. How to conquer myths, blind commitment, and get results.* Association for Supervision and Curriculum Development (ASCD).

REL, 2009. No. 069. National Center for Education Evaluation and Regional Assistance, Institute of Education Sciences, U.S. Department of Education. Retrieved from: The White House: https://www.whitehouse.gov/blog/2014/12/01/building-trust-between-communities-and-local-police.

Roberg, R., J. Kuykendall, and K. Novak. 2002. *Police management* (2nd ed.). NY: Roxbury Publishing Company.

Roberg, R., K. Novak, and G. Cordner. 2005. *Police and society* (3rd ed.). Los Angeles, CA: Roxbury Publishing.

Robinson, V., C. Lloyd, and K. Rowe. 2008. The impact of leadership on student outcomes. *Educational Administration Quarterly*, 44, 635 –74.

Rooney, Joanne. 2008. What New (Young) Principals Need to Know. *Educational Leadership*, September 2008.

Rosenberg et al. 2009. Development and sustainability of School University Partnerships in Special Education Teacher Preparation. NCIPP Document No. RS-3ES.

Ross, J., and P. Gray. 2006. School Leadership and Student Achievement: The Mediating Effects of Teacher Beliefs. *Canadian Journal of Education*, 29(3):798–822.

Ross, J., and P. Gray. 2006. Transformational leadership and teacher commitment to organizational values: The mediating effect of collective teacher efficacy. *School Effectiveness and School Improvement*, 17(2):179–99.

Safi, A. and D. Burell. 2007. Developing Critical Thinking Leadership Skills in Homeland Security Professionals, Law Enforcement Agents and Intelligence Analysts Homeland Defense Journal, vol.5, Issue: 6, Dated: June 2007, Pages: 50,52, to 54.

Sanders, M. and A. Harvey. October 2002. Beyond the School Walls: A case study of principal leadership for school community. Collaboration. Teachers College Record, vol. 104, #7. Teachers College, Columbia University.

Sanoff, A. 2006. Investing in the Nation's Schools. Business-Higher Education Forum.

Schlechty P. C., and V. S. Vance. 1981. Do academically able teachers leave education? The North Carolina Case. *Phi Delta Kappan*, 63, 106–12.

School districts promote family engagement. Harvard Family Research Project, Issue school. *Irish Educational Studies*, vol. 34(1):25–42.

Senge, P. 1990. The fifth discipline. Doubleday: NY.

Sepaniou, R. 2009. Creation of a collaborative parent/teacher professional development program. Dissertation abstracts international: The Humanities and Social Sciences, 2009, 69:09.

Sergiavanni, T. 1992. Moral leadership: Getting to the heart of school improvement. CA: Jossey-Bass.

Simons & Friedman. April 2008. Seven systemwide solutions. *Educational leadership*, 65(7).

Skogan, W. G. et al. 2002a. *Community policing and "the new immigrants": Latinos in Chicago* (NCJ 189908). Washington, DC: U.S. Department of Justice, Office of Justice Programs, National Institute of Justice. Retrieved from: https://www.ncjrs.gov/pdffiles1/nij/189908.pdf.

Smith, E., D. Anagnostopoulos, and K. Basmadjian. 2007. Bridging the university-school divide-horizontal expertise and the "two-worlds pitfall." Fairfield University, retrieved on September 13, 2015 from: http://digitalcommons.fairfield.edu/cgi/viewcontent.cgi?article=1000&context=education-facultypubs.

Smith, S. M., and M. G. Aamodt. 1997. The relationship between education, experience, and police performance. *Journal of Police and Criminal Psychology,* 12(2):7–14.

Spiro, J., M. Mattis, and L. Mitgang. March 2007. Getting Principal Mentoring Right. The Wallace Foundation.

Stevenson, Z., and P. Shetley. 2015. School district and university leadership development collaborations. 20 (1/2), 169–81.

Stewart, D. W., & Shamdasani, P. N. (1990). *Focus groups: Theory and practice.* Thousand Oaks, CA: Sage Publications, Inc. Thousand Oaks.

Storlie, C. 2015. Retrieved from: www.military.com.

Sullivan, J. 2011. Global leadership in higher education administration: perspectives internationalization by university presidents, vice presidents and deans (doctoral dissertation). Retrieved from: ProQuest Dissertations and Theses database (UMI No. 3445264).

Szczesiul, S., and J. Huizenga, J. 2014. *Improving Schools*, 17(2):176 –91.

Taylor, Ralph. "Fear of Crime, Social Ties, and Collective Efficacy: Maybe Masquerading Measurement, Maybe Déjà Vu All Over Again." *Justice Quarterly* 19 (2002): 773–92.

Terrell, S. 2011. How global leaders develop (doctoral dissertation). Retrieved from: ProQuest Dissertations and Theses database (UMI No. 3432281).

The Danish Government. April 2014. The National Reform Programme, Denmark, 2014. Retrieved from: http://ec.europa.eu/europe2020/pdf/csr2014/nrp2014_denmark_en.pdf.

The IRIS Center for Training Enhancements. 2007. Serving students with visual impairments: The importance of collaboration. Retrieved on September 13, 2015 from: http://iris.peabody.vanderbilt.edu/module/v03-focusplay/.

Tienken, C., and C. Mullen. 2016. Education Policy Perils. *Kappa Delta Pi.*

U.S. Department of Justice. 2009. A guide to disability rights law. Retrieved September 3, 2015 from: http://www.ada.gov/cguide.htm.

U.S. Department of Education. 2001. The No Child Left Behind Act, Public Law 107 –10.

U.S. Department of Health and Human Services. 2000. Retrieved from: www.hhs.gov.

Van Reusen, et al. 1994. Self advocacy strategies for education and transition planning, KS: Edge Enterprise. Retrieved September 9, 2015 from: http://www.ku-crl.org/sim/strategies/advocacy.shtml.

Vernon-Dotson, L., and L. Floyd. 2012. Building Leadership Capacity via School Partnerships and Teacher Teams. *The Clearing House*, 85:38 –49.

Vodde, R. F. 2009. Andragogical Instruction for Effective Police Training. Amherst, NY: Cambria.

Walde, R., D. Bundeswehr, and R. Schwartzman. 2011. Military Revies, November-December 2011, 57–62.

Wallace Foundation Report. 2016. Improving University Principal Preparation Programs.

Wallace, M. 2009. Making Sense of the Links: Professional Development, Teacher Practices, and Student Achievement. *Teachers College Record*, 111.2:573 –96.

Wanat, C. L. (2010). "Challenges balancing collaboration and independence in home-school relationships: Analysis of parents' perceptions in one district." *School Community Journal*, 20(1), 159-186.

Warner, C. H. 2010. Emotional safeguarding: Exploring the nature of middle-class parents' school involvement. *Sociological Forum*, 25(4):703–24.

Wasonga, C., B. Rari, and Z. Wanzare. 2011. Re-thinking school university collaboration.

Waters, J. T., R. J. Marzano, and B. McNulty. 2004. Leadership that sparks learning. *Educational Leadership*, 61(7):48–51.

Wehrman, M. M., and J. DeAngelis. 2011. Citizen willingness to participate in police-community partnerships: Exploring the influence of race and neighborhood context. *Police Quarterly*, 14(1):48–69.

Weiss, H., and N. Stephen. May 2009. A new vision for family, school and community partnerships. Harvard Family Research Project.

Wells, W. et al. 2006. Neighborhood residents' production of order: The effects of collective efficacy on responses to neighborhood problems. *Crime & Delinquency*, 52(4):523–50.

Westmoreland et al. July 2009. Seeing is believing: Promising practices for how school districts promote family engagement. Harvard Family Research Project, Issue brief, 1–16.

Whitaker, B. 1997. Instructional leadership and principal visibility. *The Clearinghouse*, 70(3):155–56.

Williams, Steven. 2012. How Will Social Intelligence Influence a Police Officer's Interaction with the Public by 2020?

Wilson, S. 2104. Innovation and the evolving system of U.S. teacher preparation. *Theory into Practice*, 53.3: 183.

Xu, Yili, M. Fiedler, and K. Flaming. 2005. "Discovering the Impact of Community Policing: The Broken Windows Thesis, Collective Efficacy, and Citizens' Judgment," *Journal of Research in Crime and Delinquency* 42: 147–86.

Young, A., A. O'Neill, and G. Simmie. 2015. Partnership in learning between university and school. *Irish Educational Studies*, Vol. 34(1):25–42.

Zeichner, K., Bowman, M., Guillen, L., & Napolitan, K. (2016). "Engaging and working in solidarity with local communities in preparing the teachers of their children." *Journal of Teacher Education, 67*(4), 277-290.

Zemsky R., and J. Finney. 2010. Changing the subject: costs, graduation rates and the importance of rethinking the undergraduate curriculum. *Harvard Business Review*, May 2010, 301–303.

Zhang, D., et al. 2010. University faculty knowledge, beliefs, and practices in providing reasonable accommodations to students with disabilities. Remedial and Special Education, vol. 31, n. 4.

About the Authors

Dr. Fern Aefsky has more than thirty-five years of experience as a teacher and administrator in public schools. She has been an adjunct professor in special education and educational leadership in various universities. She retired from New York as a school superintendent. Her area of specialization is system change, educating at-risk learners, and creating a community culture through building partnerships. She has taught masters and doctoral level classes in special education, school law, and educational leadership. Research interests include engaging the community to increase student achievement, transformational leadership for sustainable system change, and engaging all learners.

Dr. Lorrie McGovern: DBA, Marketing—Argosy University; MA, Organizational Management—Tusculum College; BS, Organizational Management—Virginia Intermont College. She is the associate dean of the Donald R. Tapia School of Business at Saint Leo University and an associate professor of business administration. Her research interests include entrepreneurship, economic development, and academic excellence.

Dr. Sereni-Massinger has been a professor for twenty years. She currently serves as Saint Leo University's associate dean for the School of Education and Social Services as well as a professor of public safety administration (graduate criminal justice). She has also served as Saint Leo University's regional academic director for the State of Florida and as associate chair of undergraduate criminal justice. Her teaching awards include: Distinguished Faculty Award in 1998 and Outstanding Faculty Award in 2011. Dr. Sereni-Massinger has published and presented at both the national and international level on the customization of on-ground and on-line classroom environments to fit various learning styles. Her research explores the most effective teaching strategies for the on-line learning environment including the use of reality-based scenarios as an active learning tool.

Dr. Susan Kinsella is the dean of the School of Education and Social Services, formerly the department chair for human services, director of the Graduate Human Services Program, and regional academic director for Saint Leo University. She has over twenty-five years of teaching and administrative experience in higher education, having developed programs in human services and having taught in undergraduate and graduate schools of social work and human services in Pennsylvania, Florida, and Georgia. Kinsella is the author of several articles on quality daycare, competency of child welfare workers, service learning, and community collaborative opportunities in human services.

Dr. Jodi Lamb spent more than twenty-eight years working in three different public school districts and held positions that ranged from media specialist to staff developer to principal. She served as a school or district administrator for sixteen years. She worked at all levels K–12, both traditional and alternative, and served as an adjunct in graduate education for several universities before coming to Saint Leo University full-time. Dr. Lamb is the associate director of the education department and is an associate professor for the Educational Leadership program.

Dr. Denise Skarbek is professor in the Education Department at Saint Leo University and director of program approval, where she teaches coursework in exceptional student education and oversees the education department's teacher accreditation. Her research interests include youth violence, sexual abuse, special education, and teacher education, particularly in the areas of teacher reflection, safe schools, and technology and its impact on children with special needs.

Dr. Toni Zetzsche earned a BS degree in criminology, a MA degree in early elementary education and a PhD in educational leadership. She has worked fifteen years in public schools as a teacher, assistant principal, and principal. Currently, Dr. Zetzsche is a school-based principal at River Ridge High School in Pasco County. She has been an adjunct instructor in IHE and a key participant in partnership projects.

Dr. Karen Hahn is the assistant vice president for Learning Design and a professor of education at Saint Leo University. She holds a BA in psychology and elementary education, a MS in special education, and a PhD in curriculum and instruction. As a K–12 educator, she held a variety of positions including elementary education teacher, teacher of specific learning disabilities at a middle school, elementary assistant principal, and director of human resources. Her research interests include utilizing technology with children with autism and utilizing technology to increase student engagement in online courses.

Dr. Renee Sedlack earned a BA in elementary education, a MA in early childhood education, and a PhD in educational leadership and policy studies. She has worked forty-two years in public schools as a teacher, assistant principal, principal, and human resources director. Currently, Dr. Sedlack is an assistant professor of educational leadership at Saint Leo University. Her research interest is in using technology to close the achievement gap among underserved youth.

Frank Mulhern, a former classroom teacher and youth development professional, developed parent advocacy programs and promoted parent involvement in school board roles and activities by assisting parents to reclaim their children through positive parenting skill development programs. He is the founder of the Mid-Hudson Coalition for the Development of Direct Support Practice, an organization dedicated to assisting frontline workers, including teacher assistants, in the continuation of their professional and academic careers. He retired as the director of Pupil Personnel Services where he helped develop positive school and community relations through parent involvement programs, including Parent University, Sessions for Parents of Children on the Autism Spectrum, and a Special Education PTA.

Dr. David Paul LaRoche has been the principal of Hudson High School in Pasco County, Florida, for the past ten years. As member of the Hudson community, he takes great pride in the fact the he graduated from Hudson High. Prior to becoming principal, he was an assistant principal for seven years at two different high schools.